3-13-12

# Making Friends, Keeping Friends

JANICE W. HEARN

# Making Friends, Keeping Friends

A DOUBLEDAY-GALILEE ORIGINAL
DOUBLEDAY & COMPANY, INC.
GARDEN CITY, NEW YORK
1979

ISBN: 0-385-14900-X
Library of Congress Catalog Card Number 78-22231

To Nancy,
my first friend, at age five
to Peg,
my newest friend
and,
to each one of you,
who
during the thirty-five years between,
have chosen
to call me friend.
I praise God
for *you!*

# Acknowledgments

With a little help from my friends . . .

This book was written with *more* than just a little help from my friends. Almost everyone I know has helped in some way.

Some have been encouragers: Patty Wickstrand and Christy Zatkin have listened, shared, and stimulated my creativity when it's lagged. Some have given me ideas: Walt Crewson set off my thoughts about the back door; Bill Mueller aided my thinking processes in the chapter on touch. Some have provided for my needs: Gordy Hess trusted me with his library; Dave and Karen Knab loaned their house while on vacation so I could write the first draft; Florence Gilfether, church librarian, gave me a place to finish the writing when she offered the use of the library; Bill and June Huntridge allowed me to rent their cabin for solitude times; my sisters, Marge Walter and Jo Riffle, who are also my friends, helped with last-minute details.

Still other friends have shared their stories with me and allowed me to pass them on to you—in some cases with names and places changed—but with the excitement and warmth of real people left in.

My family has put up with less "wifing and mothering," a few dirty socks, and some late dinners.

But this is just a beginning. The words I put on paper cannot express my thanks for the people in my life. Friends have cared for me, influenced me, taught me, altered me. In the process, they've helped to shape my life, and have helped to make this book possible. I'm grateful.

JANICE W. HEARN

# Contents

# PREFACE

## How Did We Get Here?

Etched deeply in my memory is a road in Georgia. That frightful little road stretched knife-straight right down through the state. Tall trees grew right up to the shoulders of the road, which was so narrow that I suspected two cars could not pass if necessary. It was night, the blackest night I've ever seen or imagined. The only sound to compete with Neal's snoring and the children's occasional stirrings in their sleep was the pounding rain on the windshield. Mile after mile I drove on, growing more jittery by the minute while the only change of scenery was the number of white wooden crosses perched along the roadside—one here, five there, then three— to show where people had been killed in accidents. That road had claimed more than its share of human lives.

I drove it only once, but for twelve years I hated that road with an intensity reserved especially for it. In a sense, I personified the road, as if it purposely took those other lives, and as if the road were responsible for the fright it gave me on that dark rainy night. Only as I look back, can I understand why driving that road frightened me so, and why the fear and hatred stayed with me so many years. Long before I was aware of the loneliness and separation inside myself, that road showed me very graphically the utter terror of physical isolation. And, in so doing, it pointed me down the pathway of recognition and acknowledgment of the loneliness and alienation within.

But how did I, or how did *we*—I'm convinced that all people experience this isolation to some degree—get here? When and why did we lose track of our deep need for others and begin closing them out of our lives?

The exact when and the precise how of our state of separation is a mystery to me. I couldn't begin to come up with right answers, and I doubt that anyone could. But I think I know *why* we've not understood or been in touch with our inner needs: The vast number of changes in our society have revealed empty spots inside. We've buried our need for other people and opted for independence.

If I look at my father's life and observe what has occurred in his lifetime, I am flabbergasted. It's not only the cars, planes, appliances and such that we've acquired over the years which astound me. The whole way of life has been altered.

A few months ago, Daddy told me in a letter about constructing a crystal radio set—the first family radio—and using an oatmeal box for a case. Something about his story and the way he told it created a yearning in me to know more about his life. So I asked him to write out his memories for me. His letter in response told me about the daily schedule. Daddy grew up on a farm. The day began at 5:00 A.M., with chores such as feeding cows and horses for two hours before breakfast. Then he walked to school via the "short cut" across fields —two miles! After school there were more chores before dinner. And summer vacation from school was no vacation. There was plowing, harvesting and threshing to be done. Life was full of hard work and little pleasure, a negative aspect of what some now call the "simple life." But I think the real advantage of rural life, and probably even city life in the past, was that it centered around families. Families worked together, were tied together with common goals. And grown children stayed close to home, adding their own children to the family circle.

In contrast to the family orientation of the past, our society seems to have taken another twist. I've read predictions by experts who believe the American culture is falling apart and that families and marriage are a thing of the past.

I don't agree with such a negative viewpoint, but I do see that *extended* families are already almost a thing of the past. We've become modern-day nomads, picking up our stakes and going. Unlike the patriarchs in the Old Testament, who took their extended families and their tents along, we leave relatives, homes and roots behind.

A friend related to me how personally traumatic this pulling up stakes and going can be. Lucy had to leave her home of forty years because her husband was relocated to San Diego. Lucy told me recently that it took her well over a year to feel oriented. For months, the simple task of locating cooking utensils in her new kitchen caused her great frustration.

Besides the personal trauma, a very real frustration of mobility for many of us is the void created by the great distances between us and members of our extended families. No matter how firmly rooted we become in our adopted cities, there's still something missing. Much as I love San Diego, I'm increasingly aware of how isolated from relatives my family is. My children only see their grandparents for a week or two every couple years. And they have aunts and uncles they can't remember and cousins they've never seen. When I contrast this with my childhood and the extended family get-togethers, such as Thanksgiving—where herds of cousins and aunts and uncles and grandparents filled everybody's house to overflowing—I get lonely myself for the relatives from whom I'm separated.

Mobility has separated us from persons outside our families also. People used to have a lifetime to make friends. This was pointed out to me when I visited my father recently. I wanted to see the old family farm, and so we did the "tour." In less than two hours, Daddy and I drove to the four places he had lived as a child—all within about a fifteen-mile radius of where he lives now. When people lived in one area like that all their lives, friendships just kind of happened over time. Our mobile life-style has changed that—and along with the defenses we've put at our emotional "front doors," making friends has become more difficult, something we don't quite know how to do.

That our need for others has not gone away just because we've moved away was shown by an article I found in the March 1977 issue of *Psychology Today*.

The article reported that psychologists and psychiatrists now believe that people need to be in a larger social group than the nuclear family if they are to deal effectively with problems. The article went on to tell about an unusual therapeutic process called network intervention.

Network intervention is based on the idea that a group of friends and neighbors (and relatives if they live nearby) can work with a nuclear family that is having problems in a more efficient and more durable way than is possible by working with a therapist alone. Psychologist Uri Rueveni believes that doing this will actually keep emotional problems from reaching a crisis state, reducing the need for psychiatric hospitalization. This makes it clear that our loneliness affects us deeply—even when we don't know it's there.

For those of us who do feel isolated at times, the bigness of society intensifies our separation, yet causes us to focus on external things. And as we've looked outside ourselves for satisfaction, we've become less aware of what our inner voices are saying.

It bothers me that cities are growing larger and suburbs sprawling out over the countryside. Just five miles from where I live, there's a beautiful wild valley. I've known for a long time that it was there. But only when we decided to lease a pony for our daughter Sharon at a ranch in this valley, did I become aware of the value of close-by open spaces with trees and streams and quiet for reflection. As I've sat there in the peace of the country waiting for Shar to catch the pony—or gone trampling around the fields with Shar when Crystal's wandered far away—I've been impressed again and again with nature's beauty. Because we have so few wild valleys to which we can retreat—even "my" valley will soon be covered with houses, if the city allows—many of us never have a place where we can go to meditate upon what we do need. It's easier just to go along with the frantic rush and ignore the strange feeling of loneliness that sometimes pops up.

Then there's the problem with numbers. They make me feel categorized and fragmented. We're assigned numbers for everything: social security, drivers' licenses, insurance policies, charge accounts, employee time-clock cards, bank accounts, doctor visits, hospital stays. We can barely function without three or four of these numbers attached to our name. That frightens me. What if someday the name is dropped from the numbers? Will I know who I am? Joking about it helps a little to relieve the anxiety. We laugh about computers and how they watch over the number system. But it's no joke when the computer goes crazy. Recently, I was charged for someone else's china on a department store account. The same month the computer added our payment *to* the orthodontist bill instead of subtracting it. Yikes.

There are all kinds of other problems associated with the bigness of our society. One of the worst, I think, is a distrust

of other human beings which runs so deep that we are reluctant to even smile at another person on a downtown street.
The other day when I was walking in La Jolla, a young man
looked at me and smiled, and I smiled back. It was a warm
and delightful experience. But, normally, when I'm out walking or shopping, not only do I not smile, but I do not *look* at
others. I don't like the part of me that tells me not to be too
friendly with others, but it's there, whispering, "Danger!"

Apparently, too many of us in American society have hard-
ened our faces against this "danger" of being friendly. Philip
Slater, in the preface of *The Pursuit of Loneliness,* talked
about our facial expressions. He said that this is especially evident after being in other countries. One of the first things
travelers notice upon coming home is the number of faces
with a "grim monotony . . . hard, surly, and bitter." I think
it's sad we've had to go to such an effort to protect ourselves
from the unknown of the stranger and from the possibility of
involvement with another human being.

The fear of involvement in me surfaced recently, and the
thing I hated most about it was that by the time I'd recognized what was going on with me, it was too late for the other
person.

Neal and I had gone to the theater. One of those pea-soup
fogs which descends on San Diego periodically made the
night darker than usual, and it was impossible to see more
than a few feet ahead. We were walking through Balboa Park
after the play ended, to where we'd left the car. On the way,
we discussed the play, which we thought had been dreadful.
(Most of them we love.) I was deeply involved in the conversation by the time we came to a street and stopped behind another couple before crossing.

Suddenly, out of the fog, a little yellow Honda screeched to
a halt, only a couple inches from the man in front of me. The
guy actually had to jump backward to avoid being struck by

the car. My heart pounded wildly, and I felt breathless, stunned. Had he been hit? The man began cursing the driver of the Honda, who squealed off without stopping to make sure no one was hurt. The man continued to curse and rave as he waved his arms at the little car vanishing into the darkness. He stooped to pick up the coins that had fallen from his pocket when he jumped backward, and his wife, obviously embarrassed by his unacceptable (to her) display of anger, tried to shush him. I felt so drawn to him, wanting to reach out, touch his hand, ask if he were okay—and yet, at the same time, something inside me drew back, saying, "Stay away!" All I could manage was to weakly stammer, "Yes," when the man turned to us and said, "I was almost run down! That was really a close call!" My fear of involvement won out over my concern for another human being, and I felt terrible. I had failed to give my love, or Christ's love, to someone in need.

Maybe this tension in us between the desire to reach out and the drawing back is the basis for the great participation in clubs and organizations. I always have mixed feelings about clubs. I attended one club meeting for a year and during that time no one spoke to me or welcomed me. And in my stubbornness, I did not make the first move. Finally, I just quit going, writing the whole thing off as just one more negative club experience. Clubs, to me, somehow say we can join, belong to a group, and yet remain very much uninvolved with the others. The conversation stays on the surface, seldom penetrating to the real person inside the body. Projects and activities fill the time, and while we are there we feel less lonely. Charities and the needy benefit greatly from what we do. But it doesn't help much at all with the separation and alienation we feel deep inside, and that bugs me.

At work, where many people spend the majority of their time, some persons experience the greatest loneliness and separation. I talked with a friend who is an executive in industry about this problem. My friend said that there is no real communication, in spite of being surrounded daily by people. He feels the job situation makes it *more* necessary than usual to protect one's inner life from invasion. There's a deep sense of competition, and anything that makes one person look good automatically makes another, by comparison, look bad. So, nobody takes a chance. And this spending of energy in nonproductive competition, my friend believes, cripples the creative process in business and industry.

Another factor that causes persons to draw inward at work is that most companies and organizations have no room for failure. As a medical technologist, although I am by choice not currently employed, I can speak to that. A mistake in the medical field often hurts another human being, and sometimes endangers lives. While I believe that's serious business, maybe better called sin, I think people in the medical professions need to be allowed occasional failure and a huge helping of human forgiveness. Instead, there's a rash of lawsuit-itis pervading our society and causing defensiveness on the part of doctors and hospital employees. This might mean that the protection of the patient from harm becomes something done *really* to protect against being sued. I think there's a great sadness among persons in the medical professions these days—because to them, people's lives have top priority. No medical person wants to have to be self-defensive while he or she cares for the sick.

Is our whole society such a mess?

Some think so. They've decided it's hopeless, and have just dropped out. We all know of the dropouts of the sixties among the young. But in the seventies, and I suspect on into the eighties, the dropouts are some of the pillars of society. My husband brought me an article from his February 1977 *Iron Age* magazine. I confess that I don't normally have much interest in industrial publications. But this article intrigued me because it told about top executives who have become so discouraged and exhausted with the hustle for material possessions—and the feeling of never really getting everything one *needs*—that they are retiring years before their time to seek out a simple way of life.

It's not just the men who are dropping out. The same week I read the *Iron Age* story, an article in the San Diego *Union* said that wives and mothers are fleeing their families. In 1964 a detective agency that traces runaways had three hundred requests for locating men to every one for locating women. By 1974 more requests were received for missing wives than missing husbands.

These statistics stun me. But they tell me in a very sad way that people are recognizing the loneliness that has been growing within. The feelings of separation probably have been there, unexpressed, for a long time.

Last weekend we watched "The Grand Ole Opry" on TV, and I was touched by the expressions of loneliness in the older forms of country music. I've grown to love country music over the years, and that's a good thing because it's one of the sounds coming frequently from Neal's stereo. (What an opposite to his liking for Wagnerian opera—which I have *not* grown to love!) Somehow in the process of listening, country music has hooked me. Thinking about that, I realized that loneliness and separation have been a part of our society for some time, but only certain segments have been in touch with their feelings of isolation and expressed those feelings musically.

Trying to dredge up out of my limited knowledge of music all the types of songs I could think of, it seemed to me that loneliness has best been expressed in Negro spirituals, the blues, and in country music. I think these kinds of music touch a nerve in us because they express something we are just beginning to get in touch with, and maybe cannot fully express. Years ago, I used to listen to blues for hours—I'd put on Jo Stafford's, "Ballad of the Blues," and play it full volume all day long. It expressed what I could not then articulate.

Why did these three types of music reflect loneliness before the majority of society began to express it in any way? I could be way off base, but I think it's because the people who wrote the spirituals, the blues and country music were downtrodden and recognized their separation and alienation. They *had* to get in touch with it and express it, and so their music documented their loneliness and isolation.

Meanwhile, the rest of us were caught up in the race for upward mobility and possessions—which seemed to promise satisfaction for any inner uneasiness. We were instilled with a work ethic from our childhood. This is where I think the past life-style contributed most to our loneliness today. Parents all over the country were working hard to get ahead, and teaching their children the value of hard work. And after reading my father's letters about the way he worked, I understand why he was always urging us kids to "make ourselves useful!" Then our technological progress got hooked into the work ethic, and we became so overworked and so busy moving around the country that we didn't have time to listen to our inner voices.

Recently, I think, we've reached a point in our technology and our race to get ahead where we're discovering that these things do not fill the empty spots inside us. Some of us are saying, "Hey, wait a minute, I've had enough! What about how lonely I'm feeling? How can I find some friends?"

The people who are dropping out are saying they've had more than enough. Society has provided no answer for the isolation and alienation they feel.

But I don't believe dropping out provides an answer, either. For some it's an escape, and that's only pretending the problem is gone. For others, the attempt to go back to the "good old days" looks promising. But I think the nostalgia for the "simple life" will fade under the burden of hard work and the discovery that the lonelies follow them wherever they go.

Whether or not society is a mess, one thing I know: Society, on its own, has no answers for the age-old problem of human loneliness.

In fact, I believe that God created us to need each other. When Genesis says that God created woman because it was not good for man to be alone, it implies more to me than just the man-woman relationship. It suggests that we humans have a built-in emptiness which can only be satisfied by others.

In the beginning, people found an answer to their need for others through families. When I read the Old Testament stories I picture great swarms of people, being together. When they moved to another place, these people did so in families, taking aunts and uncles and cousins along. There was a great emphasis on family and lineage. This is shown not only by the begats, but by the fact that if a person was mentioned in the Old Testament without reference to his or her ancestors, it meant that person was a nobody. The Israelites were what we might now cynically call clanish. But as God's people they belonged together, and they lived that way. They were not isolated or separated as individuals.

And even though most of us Christians can't trace our blood lines back to the Israelites, we *are* spiritual sons of Abraham. Spiritual daughters, too! We, like the Israelites, are incomplete by ourselves. We have "empty spots," put there by God, in order that we might enjoy each other. No wonder we are uncomfortable when we live in isolation, separated from one another by the defenses we've put at our front doors.

# Making Friends,
# Keeping Friends

stupefied that this had happened to us. I just dragged myself numbly through the weekend, feeling very much isolated and alone in my worry about the problem. Easter morning I got up feeling irritable and crabby. Church was crowded and stuffy, and some lady in front of me wore a fragrance that nauseated me. All the way home from church, Neal kept prodding me, asking what was wrong with me. How could I explain the separation I felt today while my ears still rang with the sound of "The Hallelujah Chorus?" I pulled myself together and kept quiet.

By the time we'd driven to the country with our basket of chicken and goodies, I felt somewhat better. I'd resolved to enjoy the picnic. We were one of the first families there, and when the parade of my friends began, I could not understand why no one noticed that we were alone. I looked around at my family to see if we had something visibly wrong with us today. But we all looked pretty normal. The kids had all combed their hair—and we'd even all worn deodorant!

When sprinkles of rain started to fall, Neal, who'd also been feeling left out, suggested that we leave. I readily agreed. I couldn't get away from there fast enough! People were still arriving, and as they climbed the hill while we descended, with all our gear, we got some rather questioning looks. But my friends who didn't notice our separation did not notice our departure, either. All the way home I tried to figure out just what had happened. Why didn't the group settle beside us in the first place? Were we intentionally excluded? Even if it was a prearranged getting together of one of the church fellowship groups, why would someone not wave and ask us to join that group?

The answer to all my questions was the same. It didn't matter why or how; I'd been left out. The pain was the same kind I'd felt when I was six and rode my sled down the hill head first into the stone steps of my aunt's springhouse. Just as the

# ONE

## The Back Door

There I sat, on a damp, cold picnic blanket, feeling the very way I thought I shouldn't. I'd watched my friends almost stumble over my feet as they walked past me and my family to a spot about thirty feet away—where one and two at a time, they settled down into a large group. They'll ask us to join them, I told myself. But as minutes passed, and the group *over there* increased to include many of the people I know in the church, my spirits sank lower and lower. And I was not about to ask to be included, either!

Left out. Alone. Shut off not only by the people I loved— three of my best friends were over there—but closed off also from the holiday excitement. Easter Sunday, the best day of the year, the celebration of the Resurrection. And I felt as if I were still milling around, lost, in the Good Friday crowd.

I'd needed my friends desperately today. Holy week for me had been pretty unholy. I was physically tired from painting a bedroom and doing other heavy housework. Then one of the kids had an "I'm a teenager now" crisis, the first our family had experienced. It was just one of those things we parents don't believe *our* children will ever do, until they do. I felt physical lump on my head then hurt too much to cry, the emotional lump today hurt too much for tears. They wouldn't come.

And I responded to the hurt the same way I would have at age six. I retreated into myself, slammed the front door, got out the emotional bricks and cement and started to build a wall around the door. I'd show them all, I'd just close them out of my life. I wouldn't let them know they'd hurt me, and I just wouldn't ever see them again. So there!

I'd just about finished bricking up this emotional wall when it dawned on me how impractical my retreat was. Not just impractical, but impossible. I'd see some of those people in my small group, others at a class I was attending, some of them everywhere I went. Unless I moved out of town, I'd better find another way to deal with the pain. My only alternative seemed to be telling my friends how deeply hurt and alienated I felt.

That night I tossed and turned and slept little. Monday morning I was tired and red-eyed, and still didn't know just *how* I could face my friends. I drove to the beach and walked there most of the morning. I kept trying to think of a nice way to say what I felt, but there was nothing nice about it. Then I tried to think of an excuse to avoid going to my small group meeting that afternoon, and almost decided just not to show up. But inside I know that procrastination would only make the telling more difficult.

So, I dragged myself reluctantly to group meeting, still uncertain about what I would say. Once there, I momentarily considered going back behind the wall and just emotionally shutting out my friends—let them think nothing was wrong. Instead, I sat down and bawled and blurted out the whole story—about unholy week and my need for friends on Sunday and that I felt left out and let down and separate.

My friends were surprised, not by what I felt, but because

they'd not noticed my separation and my need. I'd retreated and started the wall building so quickly that my friends hadn't even had a chance to see the wall going up. In a sense, I'd *chosen* to be lonely—by expecting my friends to "read my mind" and meet needs they did not know existed. They, busy with families and friends, really hadn't noticed that I was not included in the larger group. My pain and alienation fell away as I expressed it and as I understood, too, the other side of the story. I felt loved and a sense of belonging. Easter sunrise lit up my life in the middle of Monday afternoon—the beauty of the Resurrection Day more spectacular because of its belated arrival.

Because I could put down my bricks and cement and look beyond the emotional wall before it was completed, reconciliation with my friends was possible.

My ability to see beyond the wall in this situation, though, was not because I have some super talent to see through walls —but because in the past few years, when my friends have not been able to get through the defenses at my front door, they've come through the back door instead and cared for me even while I was busy putting up bricks out front.

This experience reminded me of a poster I once saw. The poster caught my eye because it portrayed a castle, and I tend to get caught up in romantic dreams of what castle living must have been like (even though I know that castles were cold, drafty and without facilities which I consider absolute necessities). This poster castle intrigued me further as I looked at the details. Out front there was bedlam: catapults, boulders, arrows, men scaling the walls on ladders, smoke billowing from pots of oil, people on the top fighting off the attack. But at the back door there were no signs of battle. A little man, unarmed and without armor, hesitated in the doorway. His words, captioned in small print, were: "Hello? May I come in?"

As I reflected on my attempt to build an emotional wall, it occurred to me that most of us are probably a lot like that castle. A castle is a fortified home. Though castles are of little interest to modern life, they do illustrate the human need for safety. And just as today we try to protect our physical homes with locks and bolts instead of stone walls, so we attempt to defend our inner lives by securing an emotional front door.

There are many ways to defend this emotional front door. The emotional wall I build when I am hurt or threatened is really the coward's way: just retreating and licking my wounds in angry silence.

Another silent method of defense doesn't require wall-building, or involve anger. Some people just close the door tightly and deny the reality of a painful situation. For example, a man may stay at the office long into the evening hours. In this way he avoids facing the fact that communications with his wife are troublesome or that his children are noisy and bothersome. He just screens out his whole family.

Other front-door strategies are not so silent. People who see others as the cause of their inner problems usually put the defenses way out front—like land mines. The trouble with land mines is that they're hidden, and you never know where they are until you step on one. I stepped on somebody's land mine once in a committee meeting. The meeting was progressing nicely, with lots of dialogue, and it seemed we'd soon be done. As I was suggesting what I thought was a rather brainy solution to the problem at hand, another woman turned to me without warning, finger shaking, and shouted that the whole problem with the blankety-blank committee was *me*. I had no chance for defense, and so I suffered the full brunt of her attack. It took weeks before I could see beyond my own pain to understand what had happened. Only when I realized that lady's real enemy was inside herself, and not me, could I forgive being blown to pieces that way.

Someone who is shy might defend his or her front door by hurling verbal boulders. A shy person often feels inadequate and afraid of others, and so will manufacture great boulders out of injured self-pride. I used to do this, and it was quite unintentional, at least on the conscious level. My past feelings of inferiority made me super-critical of others whom I thought were better than I. The critical remarks lobbed regularly at others kept them at a safe distance, and from my point of view, kept them at the same low level where I believed I was.

Others, who find strength in their rational abilities and logical thinking processes, sometimes are quite aggressive in their defensive tactics. For these people, all truth lies in the rational and in objective facts. Everything has to be proved, almost as if life were a scientific experiment. If feelings surface, they're covered up and relegated to the category of being childish. Anything that smacks of emotionalism or feelings in other persons brings out the defenses at the front door. The machine guns are set up, and the battle is an offensive one. The intruders are run off before they even get close.

The most destructive front-door defense is stored up anger, and some people use it like a nuclear weapon—to destroy everyone around. The anger may build for years, festering as it grows. It gets triggered now and then by situations that may be quite unrelated to the reason for the anger, and ka-pow! some of it blows off. Everywhere the person goes there are explosions—at work, at home, at church.

These are probably only a few of the possible defenses for the emotional front door. They aren't very attractive, and most of us would rather not admit they're there. It's easier to see them in others, at least the more noisy and obvious ones. Some of the silent defenses remain unnoticed by everybody. Most of us are guilty of using one or more of these defenses to protect the front door. And no matter what the method we use, the effect is the same: If anyone wants to get into our inner life, he or she must go through the back door. Going through the back door is the way past the defenses, the only way inside.

My friend Walt shared with me the story of how others came through the back door into his life.

Walt is in the electronics business, and he has the brain to fit his profession. He's intelligent, a think-before-acting man. He's the kind of person who can walk into our family room, take one look at Neal's nonfunctioning stereo turntable, and say, "Oh, I can fix that." When I first met Walt eight or nine years ago, I thought he was *all* brain. He wasn't allowing the warm and affectionate person he is to be seen.

Walt learned early to defend the front door of his life with the machine guns of rationalism. So concentrated was his resistance against the people whose only motive seemed to be scaring or shaming him into turning to Christ, that he did not question even who Christ was. By the time he started college, Walt was a confirmed atheist—or so he thought.

Much of his defensive energy was spent in trying to keep the "J.C. boys" from beating down the front door. Walt imagined his immortal soul dangling from the belts of the "J.C. boys," like a scalp being counted as another victory, for themselves. "I think I could have gone through the rest of my life immune to that approach," Walt told me, "and darned proud to be able to resist."

It was the people who began to come through the back door of Walt's life who finally began to get behind the defenses. It started with his wife, Anita. He fell in love with her, only to discover when it was too late that she was one of those *ugh!* Christians. He told her in very definite terms that he wanted to hear "absolutely zero about that stuff." Anita didn't argue, and quietly attended church alone on Sunday mornings. This surprised Walt. He'd expected an attack.

When their first child was born, Walt consented to having her baptised, and went along to watch. In this way he met a few others who rattled the back-door knob. The pastor of the church discovered Walt's musical ability and asked him to lead the Christmas cantata. Walt accepted the challenge, in part at least, because he respected the pastor's intellectual sermon. Then, as Walt led the practices and the performance of the cantata, he discovered that he was not met with pressure to be converted as he had been in the past. He was accepted by the people *as if he already belonged* in that church. And that really made him wonder what was going on.

But then Walt was promoted and got more deeply involved with his job. Long hours of work, along with ulcer symptoms, drew him slowly away from the tenuous new relationships. Anita joined a woman's group in the church and gave up on him, he thought.

Two years later they moved to California. When they attended church, Walt once again felt defensive, and loaded up the machine guns at the front door. And, through the back door, came people asking not, "Are you a Christian?" or even, "Are you Presbyterian?" but *inviting* Walt and Anita to a couple's club retreat. During the retreat, in small groups, Walt saw others being accepted as they were—even when they cried. This made him begin to feel safe. Maybe he was acceptable, too. Someone put an arm around his waist, and he could talk a little for the first time.

Since then, it's been two steps forward and one back, Walt says—and sometimes no steps at all. But when others came through the back door, Christ came in, too. Walt has been drawn out of his solitary confinement behind the defenses, and he's glad to be out.

Walt doesn't think his story is simply an isolated account

about a lonely guy, who, with a little help from his friends, learned to trust others enough to let them into his life. He feels that his experience is related to all humanity and that, in spite of the clammering for privacy and independence, people have a deep longing for involvement with other persons.

I agree with Walt. But if there is one place in our society where we *should* be able to go for comfort and for relief from the isolation and alienation we've discovered within ourselves, it is the Church.

# TWO

# Needed: A Back-door Strategy

Eleven years ago, Jim Creswell was newly divorced. He had two little girls to raise and no friends. He was alone and extremely lonely.

Only a church "goer" at the time, Jim looked at the people around him in the pew, and found five others who were in situations similar to his. Together they developed a program, called the Dolphins. Today the Dolphins has over six hundred single persons on the mailing list.

The Dolphins Club has been good for Jim. It brought him out of his shell and helped him to grow as a person. He made new friends and no longer felt alone. He joined the church, became an active member, and now ushers for worship services.

Jim is enthusiastic about the Dolphins as part of the church program. He sees it as a place to meet that offers an alternative to the simply social singles' clubs and bars. Because the Dolphins is under the umbrella of the church, many singles have been drawn into church membership through the group. Jim feels the Dolphins, as people, have contributed a lot to the church while reaching out to lonely human beings.

But, there is another side to Jim's story, and here his enthusiasm for the church wanes. Jim believes that all churches are backward in handling singles. For many, church is the coldest place they can go. Singles, Jim says, are a special group. Whether they've never married or have been divorced or widowed, they live in a different environment. People who are married, Jim says, do not get involved enough to really understand—no matter how good their intentions may be.

Jim does believe that all this is beginning to change a little because of the vast number of single people. (It's starting to change right in my own church, with special classes and ministries for singles.) But, meantime, life for the single person is a very lonely world. It's been tough for Jim, and he is an outgoing person who makes an effort to get around and be friendly. Those who are not outgoing personalities feel their isolation more deeply. And the church isn't helping much.

But, singles are not alone in being inside the church and still feeling lonely. Because of my Easter Sunday experience and a few similar situations, I've discovered that the church does not eliminate the problem of loneliness and alienation.

Many of us have times, at least, when we feel totally left out. For me it is like being half in and half out of the Body of Christ. I am physically there with the others, but I feel as if there is an invisible circle drawn around those in the center— the in-crowd—and there I am on the outskirts peering in like my kids when they press their noses flat against the kitchen window and strain to see what goes on inside.

For those like me, who thought we *should* never be lonely again once we belonged to the Body of Christ, being separated is pure agony. In a way, I think isolation is more difficult for us than if we'd never expected or experienced relief, however temporary, for our loneliness. We *know* what we're missing!

For those who have just come to church and never really

felt they belonged at all, the problem may be one of rather undefined uneasiness or emptiness. It may not surface or be articulated as loneliness. But they, too, know something's wrong or missing, and that hurts.

I believe much of this problem arises out of the tendency to think of the church on the institutional level, as congregations and boards and committees progressing right up to the national headquarters. As such, the church has a mission emphasis that goes around the world: all kinds of programs, plans and offerings. This, of course, is doing what Christ commissioned us to do, and I'm all for that. We've tried, though, to carry this proclivity for programs down into the congregational level. It sounds good: If it works for the world, why not for our little part of the church?

It does work to a certain extent. One of the great things about programs and plans is that they enable us to provide a *place* for the Body of Christ. This is important not just for the people of the church, but for the people in the neighborhood around us.

The importance of place is beautifully illustrated by The La Jolla Presbyterian Church. We now have an established reputation among the needy in the area, which extends all the way to downtown San Diego: "If you need something, go up to La Jolla to the church across the street from the tennis courts. They'll help."

Fred Williams, our business administrator, told me how we came to be known as a place where help is available. One night after a late board of trustees meeting, a man approached the group leaving the church and asked for a place for his family to spend the night. A couple of the trustees reached down into their own pockets and provided enough to cover the family's immediate need. But the request started the wheels turning: "What this church needs is an emergency fund so that we're able to help out at times like this."

Through the board of deacons an emergency fund was established. An attempt is made to help everyone who walks into the church asking for help. The receptionist and secretaries see that the person in need is sent to Fred, who tries to sort out the specific need. If someone is hungry, they're sent to "Harry's," where the church has an account, for a meal. Some have been fed several times, Fred says. "We talk about feeding the hungry—we can't turn away the hungry who come knocking on our own door." On rare occasions where there is a need for a place to stay overnight, Fred takes the person or family to a motel and the church picks up the tab. (Naturally, all of this is done with care in order to avoid the person who might want to take advantage of the church's generosity.) One elderly man who cannot read or write brings his important papers and letters to Fred. Fred reads them aloud for the man, and signs beside the "X" when a signature is necessary. Sometimes a person will come in just to talk, and Fred spends hours trying to counsel them and show them a way out of financial problems. If the financial needs are for more than just temporary help, Fred sends the information to the board of deacons for further consideration. If the needs are spiritual, the person is sent to a pastor—if emotional, to our Center of Growth for psychological counseling.

Thus, our church program has provided a place for the needy of the neighborhood and the city. But what about those who need in a different way—those who need friends? Such people will not come knocking on our door and ask for help. They will not wear a sign letting us know they have a problem. Probably the reverse is true: The persons who feel isolated will do everything they can to hide it from us, because it looks as if *we* all feel that we belong and they don't.

What do we say to these people? What do we say to the family mourning the death of a young woman who went home from church one Sunday morning and took a drug overdose? What could we have said to the girl that would have made a difference? What do we say to a young man who attended worship services for four years before anyone spoke to him?

What do we say to people, like my sister Marge, who attended a church for eight months and only one woman was friendly enough to invite her into her home? Marge admits she's a loner, that she doesn't communicate or share her problems easily. But, she *did* make an effort to participate in the church's programs. She was on the bowling league, and while bowling, people spoke to her in a friendly way, but their concern did not go beyond a dutiful "Hi," when Sunday morning came around.

Another problem with programs is that they can tend to make the church into a social club. To some, this is comfortable because it keeps others at arm's length. Because of our defenses, letting another person get close to us is a little scary even when we desire it. So, our programs keep us just far enough apart that we don't have to touch too much. It's like wearing big rubber inner tubes around our middles.

Besides being way off base from where we belong as the Body of Christ, the social club atmosphere gives us an air of phoniness. One man I know used to be extremely active in the church, and then just quit coming. I wondered why, but hesitated to ask because I feared he might think me nosy. Finally, I gathered my courage and asked. He answered quickly and forcefully, "Because the church has become a social club and it's full of phonies. I see a guy in the bar Saturday night with a girl and then sitting in the front row pew the next morning with his wife." While the church is made up of humans and most of us still have our favorite sins, I think he made a point. When we become too programmed, we become nothing but a social club. And a social club within the church will not offer any more help for the problem of loneliness than society itself can give.

There are times when programs somehow transcend their primary intent—to teach, to get people into the church, to raise money, or whatever—and begin to reach persons where the needs are.

This happened last summer when my daughter Diane went on a backpacking trip sponsored by our church's junior-high program. She left a typical teenager: not wanting to help around the house and arguing with every word I spoke. She came home a different person. When I started peeling pota-toes for dinner that evening, she walked into the kitchen and offered to help. She made a contract with her sister to stop fighting, and she was just generally pleasant. Surprised, I asked her what had happened on her trip. Diane's answer choked me up, "I've found God."

Out of something that began primarily as a program to get kids to have fun and draw them to the church, Diane made a commitment to Christ. I asked her why.

"It could have been just another camping trip," Diane told me. "But the people who were there from the church really made a difference. There was a special guy named Dave, one of the counselors. As we hiked, he'd walk with me and answer my questions. I needed to feel that someone understood me, and Dave did. He didn't just talk—he had so much to say about Jesus. Because of Dave, I wanted to commit my life to Christ, and I grew more in that one week as a new Christian than I might have grown in a year."

It's now a year later, and Diane's commitment has lasted. She's an avid Bible reader and really desires to become more deeply Christian. Her teenager crises still occur, but they are tempered and punctuated by her growth as a Christian per-son. Thanks, Dave, for understanding my daughter, and for telling her about Jesus when she wasn't able to hear me.

Many, if not most, of our junior-high programs have similar outcomes. The growth of the department speaks for that. The group has outgrown the Sun House where the young people normally meet, so that fellowship meetings are now held in the church recreation hall. I think that's a beautiful indication that our youth leaders and counselors are really meeting the needs of the kids.

But there are times when something quite the opposite occurs: The program remains simply a program. Once we went to a banquet because we thought it would be a time to learn more about the junior-high program, to hear what was going on, and maybe even discuss some ideas we had which might be helpful. Instead, it was a dinner to raise funds for meals served to the kids before fellowship—and it never got beyond that. The purpose was good, but the people sponsoring the fund raising took so long with the "commercial" that there was no time for expressions of need or dialogue of any kind between counselors and parents.

Thus, programs by themselves do not offer relief for the problems of loneliness and isolation that people in the church might experience. Programs leave us with a sort of mixed bag. When they transcend to the personal level, programs are helpful in reaching people where they are needy. But left to their own, programs are just another meeting to attend. I suspect that programs sometimes even *increase* feelings of alienation and separation because people become aware that the church does not necessarily help them find an answer for the problem.

Penny's story shows the church at its best: hearing the need and responding to it. Here, in Penny's own words, is her story:

It all started when I thought I had the flu. But as the week wore on, my temperature climbed, the headaches got worse, and by the fourth day, my surgeon husband got worried. The internist who checked me decided I'd be better off in the hospital—not that I looked hopeless, but doctors really get nervous when they have to treat other doctors' wives.

The high fevers continued. About six times a day I got chills and shook violently. Next, I'd get very hot as the fever climbed, and then a drenching sweat would completely soak the bed. I was uncomfortable and unhappy, but completely trusting that the doctors would find out what was ailing me and simply apply the necessary medicine/surgery, and presto, I'd be well.

Besides, I wanted to get well. We'd been planning a trip to Cabo San Lucas in Baja, California, for months. It was to be my reward for reaching my thirty-ninth birthday. We'd already paid a $240 deposit on the trip.

But it soon became apparent that I would not be well enough by the end of the month to go to Baja. Then my husband informed me that his mother was coming out from Illinois to stay with our four children. Was I really *that* sick?

I had to admit that I didn't feel too well. And so my feelings of disappointment about the trip were soon replaced by discomfort, anxiety and genuine annoyance at having to be wheeled all over the hospital to undergo a variety of tests. About two days later, the doctors decided that perhaps I needed to have my gall bladder removed. That didn't sound too exotic and glamorous, but if it worked, fine. I was getting tired of the sweats. So the day after my thirty-ninth birthday, instead of going to Baja, I was wheeled into surgery.

After a day in the intensive-care unit, I was taken back to my room on the floor. But the fevers and chills returned, and I got worse. Even though the doctors had found some evidence of gall bladder disease, they began to suspect that was not the primary cause of my illness.

Back to intensive care. The oxygen level in my blood was dangerously low, even with the oxygen mask I wore, and my lungs had fluid in them.

That was *the* night. And the church responded to my need.

Here I have to say that I am going on what others told me afterward, because at this point I stopped trying to be the doctor's cheerful wife and quit joking with the nurses. I think what I did finally was just lay back and be sick.

My husband, Bob, was scared. He was concerned both for my low blood oxygen level and for the blood cultures which were not showing any growth of bacteria. He was probably very frustrated that this whole thing was so non-surgical. I think he might have felt a little panic.

But, praise to the ever-living God, what Bob did was get on the phone and call everyone he knew who made a habit of praying—both in our own church and all over the country. One of the most comforting things for Bob was his phone call to an old college buddy, a missionary on furlough from Kenya. Paul prayed with Bob over the phone, and his prayer was not "thy will be done," but "Lord, we want you to heal Penny." Bob took great courage from that prayer. He called others who also prayed with him, and they, in turn, called other people and asked them to pray.

One of the exciting things to me is that on that particular night, there were many people who either could not sleep or who kept waking for one reason or another—a sick child or a storm—and each time they awoke they prayed for me. A friend vacationing in Hawaii woke up worrying about me, and she and her husband prayed. Another friend who hadn't set foot in a church for six or seven years because of negative experiences went to a church and sought God's help for me.

My favorite story involves a woman I've met only once, a friend of my brother's. She's about seventy-three years old, and my brother calls her a prayer warrior. He asked her to pray. She later told him that she felt blocked when she tried to pray for me. Finally, on the third attempt, when she mentioned my name, she broke out into laughter and had a complete sense of peace. She called it "holy laughter." I love her closeness to the Lord. Kind of makes me wonder if He wants that for all of us. Maybe not, but it sure would be great to be so close that you'd know when to *quit* praying for someone!

A very lovely memory for me is the presence of friends who came and stood around my bed to pray for me. I loved having them there to hold my hand. And to look up and see Gordy, Connie, Janet and Victor all smiling and looking down at me was a great comfort. The Body of Christ was surrounding me.

Through all this it has become very clear to me that God our Father is really touched and moved by our prayers, and that He is completely in charge of things.

Thursday evening the doctors decided to try just about the only drug they hadn't tried yet: tetracycline. By the next morning my fever was down to 97° and it looked as if the ordeal was over. The oxygen level in my blood began to climb, and all I had to do at that point was get a little more fluid out of my lungs, get stronger and allow the surgical wound on my stomach to heal.

That scar is really gross looking, but I love it!

Penny's illness and healing was an exciting thing to witness. To see the forces of the church mustered and people responding to her needs and her family's needs spiritually with prayer and physically, too, with food, was beautiful.

It points up to me that when we in the Body of Christ are aware of a need, we are right there doing all we can to minister to that need. And I think this is the key to whether the church helps meet the needs of people—the difference between help and unhelp. Where there is a spoken need or an obvious one, we respond. But when it comes to the unspoken needs like loneliness and isolation, any help we give is almost as if it were accidental. Instead of sitting down and plotting a strategy for reaching the lonely and alienated persons among us, we have relied on the "sometimes" transcendence of our programs to the personal level.

Maybe we've been looking in the wrong place for an answer. Maybe the institutional church and its programs isn't meant to have the answer to human loneliness in some sort of a package deal. So—how do we begin to reach out beyond the obvious and spoken needs to hear the non-articulated and stifled pleas for help among the lonely?

That's a people problem not a program problem. I believe it can only be solved by and with people. I think friendship is the answer—the solution to the loneliness and isolation people experience. Whether or not we admit it, all of us are lonely at times. We have that inbuilt need for others, and when that need isn't met, we feel separate and isolated. Just as people in the beginning found relief from their inner isolation mainly through their families (and some still do, of course), we can find relief and choose a way out of loneliness through making and keeping friends.

As Jerry Gillies pointed out in his book, *Friends: The Power and the Potential of the Company You Keep,* friends sometimes can *better* meet our needs for other persons than families can. This is because we can choose our friends, specific to the need.

Making friends, and keeping them, too, means being involved in the other person's life, getting inside, and making a difference in your friend's life because you're there.

Let me illustrate what I mean by telling you a little about how one friend has made a difference in my life.

She's a fairly new friend, and maybe that's why I'm able to see the difference so clearly. When I am with her she affects my life so profoundly that I am changed. Her reactions to me teach me why I am lonely. I'm able to discard old behavioral habits because she reflects back to me what I'm doing. Sometimes I look pretty awful: a frightened little girl, hiding; or a pushy, selfish woman, only concerned for her own needs. But the reflection of me is so colored by my friend's love that I am not threatened. I'm then able to freely choose to act differently.

And there is more. She expresses her care for me through a touch, a hug, an endearment; and in doing so, has released the bonds that have held me back from expressing affection for others. Not only do I take delight in her affection for me, I learn to express my love for other friends more freely. Having her inside my life has altered me immeasurably. She's called me forth from my isolation and sent me out to do the same for others. Just by being my friend, she's taught me to be a friend.

The process of making and keeping friends is endangered before we begin, though. As I've thought about friendship and all that is involved in being a friend and having friends, I've realized that all around me are people, who, just like me, have built up defenses at the front door of their lives—and who silently yearn for someone to get through to the person who lives inside.

When we can't get past those front-door defenses—and I don't think we ever can—we have to go around back. But how do we know how to find the way through the back door of another's life, and thence, inside?

With this question heavy on my mind one day, I walked into the family room where the children (I should say "young adults") were watching a cartoon. There was Bugs Bunny, inside a castle, at the back door! He was piling up door after door, each behind the other, in an attempt to keep Yosemite Sam—who was lurking around outside—from getting into the castle. I guess Bugs had decided to defend the back door of his castle as well as the front. At least, he was going to make certain the back door was not too easy to get through. When he'd piled up all the doors, Bugs placed a formidable looking explosive, that would go off if all else failed, right in the middle of the castle floor. Then, he left the castle. He must have been afraid of his own defense system!

The next scene showed Bugs walking down the hill away from the castle, with that beautiful swagger of his. He paused, turned to look back at the castle, and said, "I wonder if he's stubborn enough to get through all those doors?" Immediately, the castle was blown to bits.

Yosemite Sam must know something about getting through

back doors! We have something to learn from his persistence. But he certainly "blew it" by being so forceful. We don't want to follow his example in blowing the castle to bits.

Poor old Yosemite's mistake was in using front-door techniques to get in the back door.

He was like the little kid I watched the other day. I was "hiding out" in the church library to finish this book. When I went out to get a cup of coffee, I had to pass through the patio where the preschool nursery youngsters were playing. One little guy, maybe three or four years old, was in a big cardboard box. He'd taken possession. But another little fellow thought that box looked great, too, and that he'd like to share it. He said, "We'll be friends!" My ears perked up and I stopped to watch. The one who wanted to be friends was ignored. He started shouting, over and over, "We'll be friends! We'll be friends!" The other child, who apparently did not want to be friends, pushed his hand into the aggressor's face (not any too gently) and backed him away from the "doorway" on the box. But the "friend" kept pushing forward anyway—and never got in.

That's the way it is with front-door techniques. In being too forceful we almost never get "inside."

I believe there's a way in, though, through that old back door. And destruction is avoided by the *methods* we use to get inside. There can be no pushing. Instead, when we are quietly persistent, rattling the doorknob a little, asking to be invited inside, only the front-door defenses are blown to bits. The explosion is constructive, and the person inside emerges from his or her isolation.

What we need, then, is a back-door strategy. It's *method* that makes the difference and permits us to walk gently through the back door of another person's life—allowing friendship to happen.

Or, perhaps I should say, *makes* friendship happen. We

don't just "fall" into friendship. Becoming friends requires a purposeful effort. It means saying, "I choose to be your friend," and then making that happen.

But—where do we look for the methods that make friendship occur?

Apparently the methods cannot be found by looking to our culture or society. In one of the best researched books I have discovered, entitled *Friendship*, Myron Brenton said:

When I began to research this book on the meaning of friendship . . . I assumed I would work up a set of standards—a definition, as it were—of friendship. As it turned out, that intention was, if not presumptuous, at least naïve. There is no magic formula for friendship . . .[1]

A recent article in the September 1978 issue of *Ladies Home Journal*, entitled "How Good a Friend Are You?" also suggested that society has no methods or rules for friendship:

Our society tells us what husbands and wives are supposed to be and do for each other. We know what traditional obligations bind parents and children. But there is still one vast and important area of human living that remains undefined—friendship.

Most of us want and need good friends. We search for an extension of, or even a replacement for, family support. We crave the bond of absolute trust. We yearn for someone we can call in the middle of the night when we're in trouble. But it isn't always easy to achieve and sustain those relationships; there are no strict rules for how to make—and keep a friend.

In search of methods, I decided to see what the Bible has to say about making friends. Not much, in a direct way. There is no list there, either, containing "the rules of friendship." But I think scripture does teach us the methods necessary for a back-door strategy.

After all, God created us with those empty spots in the first place. I think He did that on purpose, that we might fully enjoy His other people. If we were complete in ourselves, we'd be perfectly content to wallow in isolation.

And, just as God gave us the empty spots in the first place, He gave us ways to live even in this mobile, numbered, fragmented society—with our inner needs met. God supplied the methods of making friends when He gave us Jesus Christ.

As I study the Gospel stories and consider Jesus' life, imagine Him walking among people, I see the characteristics necessary for making friends: the methods for getting through the back door.

The common denominator in these methods is that friendship is an individual matter. We can't program it or depend on the institutional church to tell us how to do it. As individuals, we can examine the methods Jesus used, and begin to develop a back-door strategy. Where do we begin?

Jesus teaches us, first of all, that we must be willing to step out of our own inner isolation. We have no right to open the back door of a friend's life and ask to be invited inside—unless we begin by taking down the defenses that we've built up around our own front doors. This means we must quit hiding who we are and risk being real.

# THREE

## Self-revelation: The First Step

When I was in fourth grade and my family moved to the country, I attended a one-room school. There, my interest in boys got me in trouble.

I never went through the "boys are yucky" stage that most little girls do. I liked boys, and always tried to show off so they'd notice me. As long as I was with boys my own age in the city school classrooms, my flirting and teasing worked well and usually netted me a boyfriend with whom I could play marbles.

But my new school was different. I thought one of the older boys was quite attractive. He must have been about a seventh grader. All the big boys used to skulk about on the side porch of the school, and after several weeks of watching them wistfully from a distance, I decided to let my affection be known. With the other girls enlisted as moral support, I staged an "attack" on the side porch. But the boys didn't think my behavior very cute. The boy I liked sneered, then growled at me to get away and stay away. I was crushed. And his putdown affected me for life, for I saw I could not *safely* express myself.

Certainly I'd learned to hide things about myself before

that day in fourth grade. But that day I first consciously realized the danger of being spontaneously real around other people. In the future, I decided, I'd have to be more careful.
Thus, on the basis of one experience, I learned to hide parts of
me *intentionally*. It was a choice that had far-reaching consequences.

Usually, though, the ways I learned to hide myself did not
come to my conscious awareness. The learning experiences
went on somewhere inside of me, and the only way I know for
certain the extent of my inner "education" is that I see the results now when so often I become aware of a vague discomfort and a lack of freedom to reveal my true thoughts and
feelings.

But I'm not unique in possessing this ability to keep secret
my inner self. I think learning to hide in response to unpleasant situations is almost an instinct in humans.

Even as far back as Adam and Eve we began hiding. Adam
and Eve covered their nakedness with fig leaf aprons. Their
physical hiding was an external sign of their inner attempt to
hide from God. In some way that is not understandable to me,
this inner reluctance to reveal ourselves, whether conscious or
unconscious, has been passed down through the centuries to
all humanity. We still learn to hide from God and from other
people, just because it seems to be the natural reaction when
we're frightened or embarrassed.

Unless this learning process is interrupted or somehow reversed, we can go on all our lives learning to be more secretive. We're exposed daily to situations and information that
encourage being unreal. One of the most obvious ways we're
taught to hide especially affects us women. There are marriage books selling in the millions telling us how to manipulate our husbands into doing what we want them to do without letting them know what we really think and feel.

Much as I disbelieve and dislike those tactics, I caught myself recently engaging in such behavior. We were going shopping. Instead of asking Neal if he'd take me out to lunch, because I really wanted to have lunch out, I asked him if I needed to eat anything before we left for the shopping center. He saw through my sideways question and asked me why I didn't just come on straight—and then took me to lunch.

In C. S. Lewis' *Till We Have Faces,* the queen wore a veil to hide her ugliness of face and spirit. She did this in spite of the tradition in the land that women go bareface. To wear a veil meant wanting to be secret. Many years passed, and the veil became the way the queen's subjects recognized her. Then, when she wanted to go into the city in disguise, she removed the veil. Her real face became her way to hide.

This story about the queen shows that there is danger involved in being unreal. We can be secretive for so long that we begin to lose contact with what is real, perhaps even to reverse the real and the unreal. And our true selves, which are at first unrecognizable to others, might eventually become unrecognizable to ourselves.

Hiding behavior is such an insidious process that it often sneaks up on us. Suddenly one day we realize we have a habit pattern that we don't know how to break. We hide when we don't even have anything to hide.

I saw this clearly in myself a few months ago in the doctor's office. Somehow I think doctors can see "through" me, and that really frightens me—even when I'm certain I have nothing to hide. So, I sat there in the waiting room and wrote down in my journal what my body was doing. My hands were clammy, I felt jittery, my stomach knotted and cramped, and I could feel my blood racing through my veins. I'd better calm down, I told myself, or my blood pressure was going to be ridiculously high by the time I saw the doctor. It was.

Although my physical responses that day were exaggerated, all our bodies do react in some way when we are unable to be truly ourselves with other people. The symptoms may be quite subtle, but they grind away inside of us and endanger our health. We actually risk illness when we pretend we are somebody we aren't. Sidney Jourard talked about this in his book, *The Transparent Self, Self-Disclosure and Well-Being*. He described a family of germs looking for a home, and suggested that the germs cannot invade *unless* a person is "prepared":

> If I were the leader of such a family of germs and had the well-being of my family at heart . . . I would wait until he [the person being invaded] lost hope, or became discouraged, or *became ground down by the requirements of respectable role-playing*.[1]

Being unreal and secretive about our inner lives is also destructive to the process of making friends. Hiding takes a lot of energy. We are so busy deciding what we will let be known and so involved with protecting the front door of our emotional life that we have no time or inclination to think about the ways we might help open the back door of a friend's life. If we even do think about helping, we do it the wrong way, by coming on as the great helper. People don't really like to be in need of help, and the great-helper syndrome only causes others to defend their front door more vehemently.

I know that *I* get very defensive when confronted with the great-helper syndrome in someone else. For a long time I didn't understand what was going on in me in this kind of situation, but a recent experience helped me to clarify my discomfort. I learned to swim last summer, and by the time I could swim a half-mile, I thought I was doing great. Then one day a woman I'd never seen before in my life stopped me at the end of a lap and told me I wasn't breathing right, and gave me detailed instructions how to correct my breathing. I really bristled, but being me, kept quiet and tried to figure out why I felt so defensive. I'd had plenty of help from the pool lifeguards and from friends who'd helped me right from the beginning. Why did I react so strongly and so negatively to this woman's help? She obviously knew what she was talking about—she was a beautiful and fast swimmer. Then I realized that I'd gone to classes and therefore asked for help from the lifeguards, and had also requested help from my friends. This woman did not even know my name and hadn't asked whether or not I wanted help. She just decided I needed it, and though I *did*, she hurt my pride. I was so proud of my newly acquired ability to swim, and her "lesson" lessened my achievement. Only with great determination, because I knew she was right, could I overcome her great-helper syndrome and follow her instructions—which *did* improve my breathing.

Besides using our energy and preventing us from being of real help to others, hiding behavior endangers friendship in another way.

To hide means that I'm responding with behavior I learned in the past. To bring that past behavior to my present friendship hurts my friend in two ways. First, I am cheating him or her by not allowing my true thoughts, feelings and responses to be known. Second, I am not responding to my friend as he or she *is*, but to a distorted image colored by past experiences which my friend had no part in building.

This became clear to me not long ago as I sat facing a new friend, chatting. She's someone I really love, and so I was enjoying our time together. Suddenly, I was conscious of being somehow afraid of my friend, and began to retreat into my little-girl behaviors. But because my friend responded to me in a very straight and clear way, I could go home and reflect and understand what had happened. I realized it was the deepening intimacy with my friend that threatened me, made me apprehensive, and caused me to want to hide myself from my friend. I recalled what I'd seen in her facial expression that day: *My* fear of intimacy had caused *her* pain. Until then, I thought of my desire to hide as *mainly* affecting me—a sin against myself. But this experience taught me that hiding is a sin also against my friend. And that puts it in a different light; adds to the seriousness of the problem.

This all leaves me with a bit of a puzzle. Being unreal is dangerous for us as persons and destructive to friendship. And it is something we've learned, either consciously or unconsciously, over the years. Why, then, is it so difficult for us to *un*learn hiding behavior—to just choose to reveal our real inner selves to those we call friend—and then do it?

This has been an area of struggle for me, probably the most difficult part of my life during the past couple years. Sometimes I wonder why I'm even trying to write a chapter about being real, because there are days and weeks when it seems I'll never find the answers to the puzzle. And even the answers I finally stumble upon might not be the right ones, or workable. I can only write from where I'm living: learning, I hope, some new habit patterns.

Over the years there have been times, sometimes very brief, where I've had glimpses of myself being liberated from this desire to hide my true self. With a few friends I've been free, and sometimes at conferences, I feel I've finally made it. I think I have finally risen above the habit that holds me, and I can choose to live freely as myself. The feeling of being liberated in this way and seeing myself not as the uglies to be hidden but as worthy to be shared is wonderful. I am exuberant in these times, and I am always certain that *this time* I will be able to preserve this new-found freedom in my daily life, in my relationship with my family, and in all my encounters with friends.

But then, somehow, without realizing it, I'm back to looking at myself and seeing some uglies and hiding them. And it's a terrible, discouraging place to be. I've been hooked by some insidious thing, and I haven't wanted to be caught, and I don't know how it happened. And I hate hiding even more than before.

I guess partly what's made self-revelation difficult for me is that I keep thinking that I have to be likable, even "right" about things. I don't like some parts of me, such as my often crabby disposition, and I don't want others, especially friends, to see that I'm sometimes not nice. And I don't want to be *wrong* about anything.

Also, I tend to think that being real means I have to reveal all of myself at all times—something like wearing a see-through blouse! Not only is that scary, but much of the time I'm not sure at all who I am, at least not certain enough to put it into words. Once when a new friend asked me to tell him about Jan Hearn, I went totally blank. I could not think of one thing to say, so I sat there with my mouth open, feeling dumb. I think actually this is not so much a lack of self-knowledge as it is a lack of *confidence* about who I am. There are so many confusions in me—sometimes even opposites. When there are opposites, I want to see only the "good" characteristics: I don't like to see laziness in me, but it's right there beside industriousness—and so are some other unattractive things, like self-indulgence!

Thus, my desire to be likable, right, and my uncertainty about myself and the polarities I see there—all make self-revelation a tremendously fearful thing. It is fear, then, that hooks me, catches me insidiously, and throws me back into my previously learned habit patterns of hiding parts of me. It's fear that sabotages my decisions and makes it impossible to implement my choice to change my behavior.

But how do I kick off the fear and be me? How do I stand up and say, "Here I am, guys, likable or not, right or wrong, and full of confusions," even when it's not safe to do that—almost *never* safe?

Rock climbing taught me about physical fear. I went on a weekend wilderness trip with nine other women a couple summers ago. I'd never camped out before, even in a tent, so to be thrown into a total wilderness experience was like going to the other side of the world. All that dirt! I've had one too many courses in bacteriology to even *consider* eating anything with unwashed hands—and here were people passing me food with positively grubby hands, and eating off the same spoons as one another! By the time we got through the first meal and were ready to climb rocks, my nerves were shattered along with my standards of cleanliness. I was really on edge, and that made me completely vulnerable to the fear I was soon to experience.

We hiked over to the area where the team of people who were to teach us climbing awaited, and I quickly discovered that rock climbing means I need to trust the person on the top end of the rope with my life. I'd never seen the guy who was at the top before. Someone told me he'd had very little experience belaying, and besides that, I could not see him now, from the bottom. But I hooked into the rope anyway, and shouted that I was ready. The jerk he gave nearly flattened me. Sheer terror! I was certain I was going to fall, flat on the front of me, and be dragged up 75 feet of granite rock. I couldn't find a place to put my feet and I was too frantic to remember to pull on the rope and signal stop. I've never moved so fast in all my life. I went up that rock like a spider whose feet are burning, screaming all the way. When I got there, I determined I was not, for any reason, going back down. I just stood there, shaking and dazed, afraid even to look down. When the leader urged me to get on the rappel rope, I begged him to show me another way down. There was only one way, of course. I'd have to face up to my fear and get on the rappel. They hooked me in and showed me there was no way the rope could possibly come undone, even if I dropped my part of it. Somehow, by facing up to my terror, my fear changed to trust. I knew I could do it. The rappel down was fantastic.

The emotional fear involved in self-revelation is different than the sheer physical terror of something like a rock-climbing experience. The emotional fear is more subtle and pervasive, and it doesn't go away the first time we face it. But each time we do choose to face up to it, it becomes less scary and easier to trust our friend to be for us and not against us.

One discovery I've made, as I've tried to face the fear of self-revelation and to learn to trust, is that it's not just I, but all of us who have opposites or polarities in our personalities. This is difficult to admit, because we'd all like to be congruent —by congruent, we usually mean all good, too—and to admit that we're not is rather unpleasant.

I first perceived this when I took a correspondence course in writing fiction. Though I never learned to create realistic characters or to write fiction, I did learn that it's necessary for each character to have at least one strong characteristic and one weak or opposite one. This is what makes him real and brings him or her alive to the reader. Just so, these opposing characteristics in ourselves, which sometimes cause us fear and confusion, are the things that bring us alive and make us real to our friends. Polarities add spice to our lives.

It's interesting to notice that Jesus, too, had these polarities in his personality. He was at times impatient and pushy with the disciples, and at other times full of long-suffering and compassion. He was caustic in his response to the Pharisees, in contrast to his gentleness with sinners. He could be deeply serious, and then show a strong sense of humor, as He did when He talked about a plank in one's eye. Jesus even changed His mind once, in the story of the Canaanite woman (Matt. 15:22–28). He first refused to heal her daughter, saying that He was sent to the lost sheep of Israel. But the woman was persistent and badgered Him until, because of her faith, Jesus healed the daughter.

But the really amazing thing about Jesus is that He did not try to hide these opposites or to deny their existence. He lived them out, as an integral part of His daily relationships. Because He could do this, Jesus was the most whole person who's ever lived. He had clarity about who He was, and didn't have to use His energies wondering about the confusions. It also gave His life simplicity and direction because He did not have to worry about the things with which we concern ourselves: what other people will think, if we look okay, what will happen if we do such and such.

I think it was Jesus' clear focus on who He was and His ability to be comfortable with His diversities within that enabled Him to see His purpose for being with such certainty. Jesus was so sure of His purpose that He could state it in one sentence: "My task is to bear witness to the truth." (John 18:37, NEB.) And He backed up his statement clearly: "For this I was born; for this I came into the world . . ." No "I thinks" and "maybes." Definite, certain and unquestionable.

As we are able to further identify the diversities inside ourselves and try to live them out and integrate them into our daily existence, just like Jesus we will become more whole. We'll be less uncertain about who we are, more self-confident and feel more sure of our purpose for being. And, like Jesus, we'll be more able to reveal our inner selves; even the opposites.

I think the best way to begin doing this is with two or three friends with whom we are already fairly comfortable. It's paradoxical that the thing we fear—revealing our true selves to our friends—is the very thing that helps to remove our uncertainties and enables us to know ourselves more deeply—thus preparing us to be even more real. Paradoxical or not, it works. Just looking inside doesn't do the whole job because there are things we hide from ourselves. We can only discover those hidden things when someone else is willing to tell us. To have a really accurate picture of ourselves, we need to add what friends see in us to what we discover in our own inner dialogue.

Patty, Christy, Karen and I did this for about two years. We'd known each other for eight or nine years, but a couple years ago we all sensed we'd come to a new dimension of friendship. We met weekly or biweekly, as our schedules allowed, with a commitment to be honest with each other on a deeper level than we had in the past. There were a lot of white-knuckle meetings, a few angry ones, some tearful and also joyful moments. It was often scary for me because this commitment constrained me—and still does, though we no longer meet formally—to behave in a different way than what I normally would. My sharing of my hurt and alienation about Easter Sunday, for example, was largely because the four of us share this covenant.

Even at times when I've worked out a difficulty in the friendship on my own, as I have recently with one of my friends, this commitment requires that I also talk to her about the problem, at the right time. Talking to her is necessary not only because I've covenanted to be honest, but because the information she receives from my sharing will aid her in *her* search for self-knowledge. So, I'll talk about what I've experienced with her, even though it scares me silly!

This kind of commitment is not all scary, though. One of the most valuable aspects of the covenant for me is that my friends see things in me from a different perspective than I do. Often I tend to be negative or self-condemning toward myself, while my friends, as outside observers, see a situation from a positive viewpoint. For example, once when I'd gotten deeply emotionally involved and hooked into a manipulative and unhealthy situation with another woman, I finally had to

end it. I had to just say, "No more of this!" I had never purposely ended a relationship before, so I was condemning myself for that and for getting involved in the first place, for allowing myself to be manipulated—and a thousand other
things. But Patty saw it another way: She thought it wonderful that I'd not allowed the involvement to continue over a
long period of time—that I'd listened to myself and found clarity and decided what to do. That kind of perspective alters
my self-image in an affirmative way, and I need it and like it!

But, facing the fear of being real, identifying and inte-
grating diversities, and covenants to reveal our true selves to a
few friends—are all just a beginning. Doing all these things is
a choice we can make, but it takes more than choice.

Being real is not something to be done merely by decision
or by will power. Though that *is* the first step, the intellectual
choice does not make it happen. As much as we desire to
break loose from the habits of repression and hiding, we cannot—unless God's power is in our lives. All our efforts can only
chip away at the surface. Somehow the desire and the choice
to be real has to get inside of us, down to the unconscious
level, where most of the hiding behavior was learned in the
first place. It takes the Holy Spirit, whose indwelling gets
down into the corners of our minds, to really change anything.

Until very recently, I believed the Holy Spirit worked only
from the inside out in changing me. But now I know He also
works from the outside in. This is why, over the years, I've
had only brief glimpses and experiences of being liberated
from my hiding behavior, as much as I wanted to be different.
Through a series of deepening friendships and some new situations, I saw, intellectually, that self-revelation was such a de-
sirable and exuberating experience that it was worth any risk
at trusting or any amount of work. I think it's important that I

had to make that choice because I don't think the Spirit could do His work until I desired it to be done.

This has been much like a death and resurrection experience for me: almost as if finally, in my struggle to do it myself, I was so stifled and turned inward that I was deadened. I wanted very much to quit hiding, and yet this feeling of deadness made me aware that I could not even be real with myself, let alone with my friends. Out of a deep inner yearning, I turned to the Holy Spirit for help, and felt life stirring within me again. I believe that through this death-resurrection process the Holy Spirit took the desire of my conscious mind and made it an inner thing, a part of my unconscious. He somehow integrated the outside and the inside and just tied it all together. The hidden habits are no longer fighting with my outer decisions to change my behavior. I am more whole.

All this doesn't mean that self-revelation will be easy from now on. I've already seen that it isn't. Establishing new patterns requires thinking out procedures and taking positive steps toward being more real.

One thing I've done so far is to try to talk more to Neal and share my thoughts and feelings with him on a regular basis, instead of keeping things to myself—or waiting until I'm angry and then dumping it all violently on him. I've found it takes great perseverance for me to *keep* doing this.

Another thing I've done is to try to become aware of the physical positions I put myself into that encourage hiding behavior. These things prevent self-revelation and keep me distant from other persons. They are rather like escape hatches from intimacy. For example, in my Bible Study Fellowship group last year, I was feeling that I really didn't know anyone very well, despite having seen those girls weekly for months. Looking at my physical behavior, I saw that sitting in the back row for lecture—so I could leave early to get out for lunch or other appointments—was keeping me from the two times in

BSF that allow chatting. Just those few moments before and after lecture, spent sitting and chatting with someone in my discussion group, helped me to get to know some of the other women.

Maybe these seem small steps to anyone else, but for me they are giant ones. Most helpful to me is just to keep reminding myself that nobody learns everything overnight. It takes time and repetition to establish trust. As Andrew Greeley says:

Instant openness and instant trust are usually phony openness and phony trust.[2]

Self-revelation is not an all-at-once or an all-to-everyone experience. It means selectively revealing a little at a time. Taking a tentative step with a friend and awaiting his or her response.

In revealing myself slowly to another, I am taking the first step of friendship—the tender, tentative step through my friend's back door. I'm saying to my friend:

"I trust you enough to care for me and like me even when I'm not at my best. And I promise to do the same for you."

That kind of trust, allowed to grow and develop, is the basic requirement for making and keeping friends.

For those of us who have spent much of our lives defending the front door by hiding our inner selves, the risk of trusting is great. So great that we may not want to chance it, especially when the liberation process can be so long, and the "rewards" seem so far in the future. The bottom line is that self-revelation is never safe. Expecting safety is not realistic. Our friends not only might, but will, disappoint us and let us down if we dare to trust them. Only God is totally trustworthy. We may even experience rejection or humiliation if we dare to reveal ourselves. Is anything worth that?

God thought so. He showed us how when He gave us Jesus

Christ, for in Jesus we see God's self-revelation. It wasn't safe for Him to be known in that way—just look at what happened. How insignificant is our disappointment, rejection, or humiliation compared to the rejection Christ suffered?

# FOUR

## Sensitivity:
## A New Way of Seeing

Several years ago the man who then lived next door came over to our front yard. Without speaking to me first, he pruned one of our palm trees. Pruning a palm is not an easy job because the main stalk of the frond has sharp projections all the way up. Trying to avoid being scratched while standing on a ladder and sawing off one frond at a time is quite an experience. I *should* have been thankful for my neighbor's help—the tree really did need to be pruned. And apparently my neighbor needed to be helpful. But what the guy didn't see was what *I* needed. One of my big needs is for space and privacy. Thus, I saw his tree pruning as an infringement on my "property rights." I also saw red!

There's a very fine line between being sensitive to another person's needs and infringing on his or her rights as a separate person. But that fine line marks the boundary between the front and the back doors. Infringement means trying to force yourself through the front, regardless of defenses. Sensitivity, instead, may be a way through the back. It's a vital part of back-door strategy.

Sensitivity is like a sixth sense. But for many of us, its presence goes unnoticed and undeveloped because sensitivity has not been one of the values cultured by our society.

Sensitivity is, first of all, an outgrowth of subjectivity. I think that's why we as people have tended to neglect this area, and therefore not known of its importance in friendship. It's not so much that we haven't wanted to be sensitive to friends in their need as it is that we are apprehensive about the subjectivity required to become sensitive, caring people.

Subjectivity causes us to be uneasy mostly because the word has a connotation of focusing on self. It suggests introspection, and that's not socially acceptable! (Often people tell me I'm too introspective, and they always *frown* at me when they say that.) I think subjectivity and introspection make people uncomfortable because both terms are translated as "the big I." People see the inward focus as an end in itself, and therefore deny the whole area of subjectivity. As a result, the focus has been turned to the objective and easily observable things of the world.

Part of this is learned, too. We've been taught that being objective and scientific is somehow better, maybe even the *sign* of a well-educated person. Perhaps it's different now—although I see no real changes in the way my children are being taught—but most of my education concerned learning facts and how to prove those facts. With my ability for rote memorization, I handled that well. And I still see the necessity for the objective in such areas as science.

I'm just saying that objectivity is not all there is to life. Because of my objectively oriented education, I didn't learn to *think* until I was thirty. I didn't know until then that I was capable of thinking! I don't believe that had to be. I see no reason why objectivity and subjectivity can't coexist. They fit together and complement each other rather than one overruling the other. Instead of thinking in terms of either/or, we can use both subjectivity and objectivity. Even in the area of sensitivity, which begins with subjectivity, there is a place where objectivity, in the form of separateness, enables us to better use our skills. More about that later.

For now, how do we begin to make the journey from a totally objective past to an orientation that includes the subjective?

For me, the journey began with commitment to Christ. I think of it as being picked up, turned around and put down again, walking in the opposite direction. It's a reversal of the way I was. And while I can see and appreciate the truth in the objective, my viewpoint has changed to include the subjective, a new dimension which I think is a more complete view of God's truth.

Sure, this subjective viewpoint has gotten me into trouble—when I've used it in my own ways. Christ is teaching me the value of looking inward, but not as an end in itself because that leads nowhere. When the looking inward is done with the goal of understanding myself that I may better understand others, something happens. I begin to be sensitive to the needs in my friends, giving my inward look a different purpose.

It's a long way from the selfishness of looking inside and staying there, to the kind of sensitivity that drags me out of the inner me and into a friend's life.

One of the things that has made sensitivity difficult for me is that I don't tend to see the problems of others as being quite as important as mine. Other people must have this same problem because I found a little verse written by Ellie Womack that expresses it beautifully:

### Life Swap

Your troubles seem quite small to me,
While mine, you say it's plain to see,
Against your beach are grains of sand;
But you, of course, don't understand

The frightful burdens that I bear
While you glide by without a care.
I wonder if we'd feel this way
If we'd trade places for a day.[1]

If we *could* trade places for a day, there'd be no problem in understanding the importance of another's troubles. We could readily identify with our friend's position, and we'd see that his or her problems matched ours any day.

But there is a way we can "trade places," even though we cannot physically get under another's skin. By continuing to deepen our knowledge of the subjective side of life, we can develop the sensitivity to "see" beneath a friend's skin.

Seeing beneath the skin of another person means not only using our eyes, but a variety of senses.

Maybe the easiest way to begin is by listening. We all listen to others—or at least we think we do. But how often is what we hear simply passing through our head without having our attention?

This is more obvious to me in relation to my kids than it is with friends, but I'm often aware that I do not give full attention to friends, either. My kids, though, are all chatterers, and most of the time they're home, all three are talking at once. I love having them share with me, and I think I'm a lucky mother that they do. But sometimes I find myself mentally shutting them off: listening, answering (What was that I just said yes to?) and reading a book or the newspaper all at once. No wonder I don't know what goes on here half the time.

The kids have learned to use this inattention on my part to get past some of the disciplines, or at least to try. When Steve was grounded recently, Diane came to me very sweetly and said, "Could Steve and I go to the shopping center?" When I reminded her that Steve was not going anywhere for the rest of that week, Diane said, "Oh! I thought I'd get you! You're always flubbing on things like that." The reason, of course, is that I do not always listen. To listen, our ears need the co-operation of our brain—otherwise, nothing gets our attention.

This co-operation between ears and brain cells requires some discipline on our part. We have to set aside all the other things flitting around in our heads—like the phone call we forgot to make, or the need to get to the bank before it closes. Funny how we remember the things we've forgotten just when we're meaning to listen to another person. But pushing aside the little mental interruptions and paying our full undivided attention to a friend will help us to hear what's really being said.

This kind of attentiveness is better than hours spent in partial or distracted listening. A few moments of quality listening communicates to our friend that we think what he or she has to say is important. But we need to be willing to disregard the time of day (or at least appear to disregard time) for this kind of listening.

For example, I once heard a pastor say that when he went visiting and was in a hurry, he'd keep his coat on to communicate that he needed to make a quick escape. But he later learned that by taking off his coat, being relaxed and offering undivided attention for the few minutes he was there, his calls actually took less time than when he tried to rush. In addition, the person called upon felt more visited because he had received total attention.

Looking at our friend when we listen—not around, through or past him or her—is very important. It helps us to focus our attention and gives the friend a sense of being heard.

Just the other day, while I was speaking to a man, his eyeballs were bouncing around like Ping-Pong balls. His responses implied that he actually heard what I said, but I had a lot of trouble believing that he had. And I'd have to go a long way to call that guy friend because his Ping-Ponging eyeballs implied that he couldn't care less about what I had to say.

Maybe we'd listen more effectively if we had more appreciation for the capability of the human ear. Part of a physiological psych course I took meant studying the ear. I never thought I'd understand it or get it straight. How complicated!

The human ear, even though complicated, is a fascinating organ. The way the air vibrations are transmitted through the ear drum to the inner fluid, the smallness of the cochlea (inner ear) in relation to the frequency of the sound we hear, the tiny hair cells that transduce the vibration to a neural impulse so it can be carried to the brain: It's all a miracle of creation.

And when we give full attention to what we hear, we quickly discover that our ears don't miss a thing. The ear is so capable of doing its task that we have learned to unconsciously tune out some of the sounds we hear. Therefore, many things don't get our attention and just escape our awareness. Knowing that, we can increase our listening ability by consciously attempting to hear more.

That we are capable of hearing more than we do was illustrated by a newspaper story about John Wickersham, a blind detective who lives in Idaho.[2] His story was told just after he'd completed his first case. He felt being blind was to his credit because he was forced to *rely* on his ears. He learned to pay special attention to a person's voice and became such a good listener that he can now tell by the *sound* of a voice whether or not a person is telling the truth.

The beauty of this story is that it shows that using our ears more effectively is only a matter of attention and practice. And by increasing our ability to listen, we've made a giant step forward in developing sensitivity, that ability to see beneath our friend's skin.

Another way of "seeing" is through our sense perceptions.

Theodore Reik wrote about these sense perceptions in *Listening with the Third Ear*. He described them as a subconscious awareness of what is going on beyond the external or the objective.

We all have these perceptive powers—a way of seeing with our subconscious mind—which we do not ordinarily use.

A television show suggested that not only humans, but all living things, have these perceptions. A scientist wired a plant to a polygraph machine to show that the plant responded to having its leaf cut. The needle movement on the polygraph made by the plant was similar to that made by a woman's reaction to having her hand cut. The scientist then went on to explain that even bacteria in yogurt seem to have perceptions beyond our imagination.

Well, I'll let the scientist worry about bacteria and plant perceptions. But I think that we as people need to become more aware of the perceptive powers within us if we are to be sensitive to the needs of our friends.

A friend told me how he was shown something about sense perceptions when he participated in a small group. The group was given a sack of lemons. Each person was told to choose a lemon and get to know that lemon. After a "get-acquainted" time filled with jokes and laughter about the silliness of the game, the lemons were placed back in the bag, mixed, and dumped on the floor. Each person was then instructed to find his or her lemon. Not one lemon was left unrecognized! So what seemed to be only a silly game pointed out to these people the potential for perception—which is often unused. And if we have the ability to see so much about a lemon, what does that say to us about people?

That these perceptive powers are available to us was shown in another way in a speed-reading course I attended. The instructor taught that persons who read fast catch the idea of the words in their subconscious. They get the point through visualizing subconsciously rather than by the meaning of each single word. It works, too. I often resist speed reading just because I'm afraid I'll miss something! But when I've risked it, I've discovered that I do get a sense of what I've read. Reading fast, at least part of the time, is a good way to develop sense perceptions.

On the other hand, the reverse works, too, in developing perception. Reading carefully the novels written by a great writer also helps to increase our perceptive abilities. Chaim Potok, for example, creates word pictures of people. His characters seem more real sometimes than actual people. This is because he helps us, by means of sense perceptions, to visualize beyond what we normally see. I like to write paragraphs of Potok's work out in longhand—as a sort of learning experience. Writing it out helps me in studying his work to see more clearly some of the things I often miss. Learning not to let things pass me by is part of what sense perception is about.

Practicing the use of sense perceptions helps, too. In a class I attended, taught by a doctor, we were encouraged to do this. We sat in pairs, facing each other, eyes closed, hands touching. Then we were told to send love to the other person. Most people in the class experienced a feeling of warmth and energy movement through their hands. Then we were told to try to block the love being sent to us from the other person. Some of us could sense drawing back; a few felt coolness in their hands; some experienced *pain* all the way up their arms. All of us were amazed. We had not known we had the ability to be so perceptive.

Still another area where we fall short in seeing involves the eyes. We think we see clearly the things that surround us, and in our better moments maybe we do see most of it. But, basically, we do not use our ability to observe.

Television advertisements take advantage of our lack of observation by using subliminal techniques. Flash views of sensual gestures attempt to stimulate us, and deathly symbols challenge us to flirt with death. And it's all done so cleverly that only our subconscious picks it up. Our eyes don't.

Observation means getting our subconscious sight and our eyesight together. This requires more than just looking at something. To observe means to catch the whole flavor or the entire picture of what we see. Even when we attempt to see the whole, we usually don't.

Recently I bought wallpaper for the bathroom. When I picked it out, I saw the colors gold, orange and green. Not until after all the cutting and pasting had been done, did I notice a second shade of green and some white. A full week later I discovered that there is a lot of beige in that wallpaper. And only by "living with" it did I discover the total effect: Its yellowness makes me look jaundiced.

Thus, it's necessary to train ourselves to be observers if we are to be able to see beneath the skin of a friend.

This training is not difficult. It just means being more alert and noticing little things. For example, one morning last week I walked past the carport twice, taking out trash. Later in the day, Steve asked me if he could drive the car wherever he was going. I actually could not remember if the car was there in the carport. I hadn't "seen" it in two trips! This is the kind of thing we humans do all the time. With a little concentration, using physical things like seeing the car, we can begin to train ourselves to see the more intangible things in a friend.

Observation like this is important in being sensitive because often what a friend doesn't do or say may tell us as much about that person as anything. Teaching ourselves to recognize unusual quietness in a friend, for example, might tell us that what she really needs is not to be silent, but to share. It might be a time when we can give her understanding and help for carrying a burden.

A few months ago one of my friends was struggling. Both

her teenaged sons were having problems, and she was experiencing great sadness. She was reluctant to share it because she didn't want to burden others. But at a meeting, a couple other women saw through her silence, observed the total picture, and took her off to the kitchen. The barriers came down and she shared the pain. Although the others could not change the situation, they could help her carry the burden. She was not left to bear it alone.

Developing sensitivity by learning to use our senses—listening, perceptive powers, observation—really does help us to get under our friend's skin and understand what goes on there. We see beyond the obvious or the objective to what the real problem is.

Seeing beyond the obvious is what Jesus did. He saw that the paralytic needed to be forgiven before he could be healed. Christ recognized the demons who caused persons to behave psychotically. Whatever the problem appeared to be, Jesus saw beyond it and gave what the person really needed.

Seeing this way enables us to notice the pain in the eyes of the carefully controlled face, to catch the hopelessness in the drooped shoulders, to recognize the dulled voice of depression. But letting a friend know that we are aware of the need is an area calling for sensitivity, too. Maybe our friend would rather we didn't know—or maybe he is still unaware of the shape and size of the problem. How do we handle this?

Jesus handled it in a very natural way, by asking for a response from the other person. In Mark 3:1-5, Jesus met the man with the withered hand. It's interesting to note that while we have been taught from earliest childhood not to stare at a person's deformity, whether it be physical or emotional, Jesus looked upon the withered hand. Then He let the man know He saw the problem. He called the man to Himself, and said: "Stretch out your hand." Presumably, if the man had not responded to Jesus' request, the Lord would have walked away. Because the man responded, Jesus healed the hand.

Thus, if we tactfully and naturally ask a friend for some kind of response and then allow her the freedom to respond or not, we eliminate guessing whether or not our friend wants to share the problem with us at this point.

There are times, though, when even asking for a response is not right. This is where sensitivity requires a great deal of tenderness and patience.

A friend, sensing the need for love in a person she'd met, told me, "I want to love her so much. But I sense that she's emotionally holding her hands out in front of herself, telling me that if I come any closer, she'll run. I finally had to decide that to love her is to not penetrate the space around her. I have to be constantly sensitive to where her space is."

A word of caution: The ability to be sensitive to a friend's needs may hold danger if we use it unwisely or irresponsibly. We are not called to be armchair psychiatrists. We can really mess things and people up if we try to function in an area where we have not been trained. Plus, who needs psychoanalyzing by his friends?

Sensitivity doesn't include trying to be the great fixer-upper or the great healer, either. It simply means developing an awareness of our friends' needs and being willing to share the load. Anybody can do that—and we all need to do more of it.

Although sensitivity can be learned by anyone, there are some who have a special gift for it. My friend Patty is one such person.

Patty's gift, like many spiritual gifts, was hidden in her weakness. For years, Patty had searched for the gift she'd been given for the good of others. During a Faith/at/Work conference, the leader of a workshop Patty attended suggested the possibility of discovering gifts in areas of weakness. Patty knew that she was overly aware of what her friends might be thinking of her, and that she often read more into their responses to her than what they'd intended. She often found she had her antennae up, looking for others to criticize her or hurt her feelings. Patty's hypersensitivity, she discovered, was based on false preconceptions, which were products of a very fragile and weak self-esteem. Because of her low esteem, she tended to be critical of her friends, which inadvertently caused her to feel "worthwhile."

Patty turned this weakness in herself over to Christ, asking Him to transform it. The weakness, which had been used in a negative and self-destructive way, was turned around by Christ to be used constructively. Over a period of time, Patty discovered she had a beautiful gift of sensitivity toward others.

Watching Patty learn to use her gift has been beautiful, too. She's learning to set aside her own thoughts, emotions and projects, and be willing to participate with the other person in his or her need. She's constantly prayerful that what she sees in her friend is by God's guidance and not by a slipping back into the old negative critical patterns. Once she's certain that what she perceives is of God, Patty's able to almost pull a problem out of a person. As a friend shares, Patty gives feedback and follows that person through the problem. She does this with softness and perception and is often able to help her friends discover the answer or the way out of the problem.

Others are helped by Patty's gift because of her participation with them where they are. It's rather like jumping into the other person's skin and living out their situation with them.

This technique of participation has value in ways we're just beginning to discover. An article in the paper a few months ago told of a psychiatrist who was successfully curing some schizophrenic patients. By talking gibberish with them, he entered into their situation enough that he was able to draw out the sane person from beneath the psychotic exterior. Another article reported that parents of an autistic child were able to turn him around. They decided not to try to make him conform to the world they lived in, but to go to his world. They spent hours imitating his actions, no matter how bizarre. In doing so, they were able to communicate with him, and the result was a normal child.

Though both these examples of participation are at levels beyond what a friendship requires, we do need to learn to participate with a friend in his or her world. This requires that we set aside our own concerns and think of the problem of our friend as being the most important on the agenda for the moment. A kind of emotional separation is also required: to be there and experience the hurtfulness of the situation with a friend, and yet not to go under ourselves.

My daughter Sharon helped me to understand this thing about separation. Our dogs were getting their haircuts, and Shar was holding Nelson still so that Neal could clip. In the process, Nelson's ear was nicked, and began to bleed. Nels didn't even know he was hurt. But Sharon, a very sensitive little girl, believing that the dog was in pain, felt his pain so much that she fainted.

Shar's experience with the dog taught me that we need to be removed enough from the raw emotion of a friend's pain that we can function. This is where objectivity has its place in sensitivity.

Without objectivity, we can become so tied up in a friend's problem that we actually hinder her ability to deal with it. This is wrong not only because it prevents her from solving the problem, but because we are thinking too highly of ourselves when we are dragged down by the emotion instead of separated a bit from it.

I say this because the times when I have become dragged down emotionally by a friend's pain are the times when I've thought I should be able to "take away" my friend's problem. It's arrogant to believe that I can relieve or prevent all trouble for my friend.

It comforts me that Jesus' disciples apparently had this problem about getting wiped out by emotion. It made me feel more human! In Luke 22:45, I was puzzled that the disciples had gone to sleep "for sorrow." (RSV) Those words weren't used in the other Gospels. Matthew and Mark just say "for their eyes were heavy." To just fall asleep when Jesus needed them because they were sleepy almost implies laziness, or at least a lack of concern. But when I looked in the Greek text of Luke, it is implied that the disciples actually fell asleep because they were *too* concerned. The Greek says they fell asleep "from the grief." That suggested to me that they were really feeling the raw emotion of what Jesus was suffering— and they couldn't take it.

I wouldn't have been able to take it, either. But I do know that only when I am able to be objective and a little separated from my friend's pain, am I able to become a positive force in the process. If we can teach ourselves to do this, we are able to truly participate with a friend because we *add* to his subjective ability to see and understand the problem—thus making a solution possible.

Developing the skills necessary for sensitivity produces results in our own lives. Once we have learned to see beneath another's skin, and then to live there with a friend, participating in his life experience—we can never be the same again.

We've begun the journey away from our totally objective and selfish past, and placed our friend into that special place we formerly reserved for self: importance. We've learned something about what being friends is about because we are finally able to be truly compassionate.

Our compassion for a friend is bound to have some results in that person's life. There are times when we can't see the difference it makes. Maybe it's only caused her to peer through the peep hole on the back door and see who's there. But even *that* is progress in the process of friendship.

On the other hand, sometimes, being the recipient of our compassion is all our friend needs. He or she opens the back door not only to the one who has tenderly and sensitively asked to come inside—but flings it wide and invites others in, too.

# FIVE

## Acceptance:
## Yes—the Final Word

Having blundered blindly into my learning and perception class with the idea that I'd discover more about how *people* learn, I was shocked to find out that we were going to study *pigeons*.

In fact, we were going to *train* pigeons.

I guess the surprise of it all intrigued me enough that I decided to stay in the class, even though it did not seem to be what I'd imagined.

Halfway through the semester, I made my way to the farthest corner of the campus where the psych lab shacks were located. There I was given a white pigeon and an hour to train, or "condition" him. Her? Let's settle for "it."

I was instructed to condition the pigeon to do whatever I wished, using Skinner's method of *successive approximation*. Not able to think of anything terribly unique to teach a rather large bird in a little cage, I decided to train "Pige" to lift its left leg.

Since pigeons almost never lift their left leg and hold it there on purpose, I couldn't sit there and wait for that to happen. Successive approximation begins by reinforcing, with food, any slight movement in the right direction. So when Pige moved one toe on its left foot, I gave a grain reinforcement. Two or three grains later, Pige began moving its whole left foot. Gradually, over a series of dispensing about one hundred bits of grain, the pigeon lifted its left leg at a fairly high frequency, and held it there about a second each time.

Pige was a smart old bird, though, and had been trained previously to turn in a circle. My reinforcements had to be carefully made to discourage circle-turning. And Pige's new trick was still very tenuous at the end of the training session. I suspect that the habit of turning in circles would still win out over leg-lifting.

Although training pigeons seemed rather silly at the beginning of the class, it proved to be a valuable experience. Through understanding and practicing the technique of successive approximation—and applying what I'd learned to humans—I discovered that people, like pigeons, learn in a step-by-step process.

But, this step-by-step process does not fit into *our* conditioning. We live daily with a do-it-now-and-make-sure-it's-right attitude. This attitude in us which requires instantness and correctness, makes acceptance of our friends difficult. Growth and changes seem to take forever. And often we see none at all.

Add to this the fact that sometimes it looks as if people are going backward.

Like Pige, who probably went back to turning circles the minute I left the psych lab, people sometimes appear to revert to old patterns or look as if they're repeating themselves.

Individual differences give us another convenient excuse for not accepting others as friends or for not accepting their behaviors once we are friends. Many of us predetermine that anyone who is not like us in thought and action is weird: to be different is unacceptable. To top this, we focus on our feel-ings for the other person: whether or not we feel an attraction often determines whom we befriend. Others are not accepted.

Armed with these conditionings and beliefs, we approach other persons, whether they are potential friends or es-tablished friends, with a yes-but attitude.

The yes we give to others tells them we will spend time with them, enjoy them, and maybe even love them.

The but following the yes lets them know that they must measure up. If they become disagreeable or ask too much of the friendship or embarrass us by not behaving according to our expectations—we reserve the right to reject them.

If only we could learn to say yes—a simple, wonderful *yes*—to others!

Yes is the final word when it comes to acceptance. And I'm convinced that saying yes to people is the most direct way through the back door and into their lives. Not only a neces-sity for making friends, but for keeping them.

Acceptance of another person requires first that we learn some of the dynamics involved.

The place to begin is with self. Only as I can accept myself —in a sense, be a friend to myself—am I able to truly accept other persons. Part of this is accepting my emotional place in life and my own growth process. When I'm able to say yes to myself and really believe that I am an acceptable person, with all my imperfections and slowness to grow, something hap-pens to my attitude toward my friends: I'm able to pass the yes on to them.

Maybe the most important dynamic concerning acceptance is that it has continuity. Acceptance is not a motionless thing. We tend, I think, to view it as a fixed moment in time. Once we've accepted someone or something, that's that. But not see-ing movement as part of acceptance gets us into trouble, because it leads us to believe that we've arrived and causes us to expect our friends to do the same.

The direction of the movement is important, also. Understanding this is easier if we take the human-growth process with all its tottering and tenuous steps and imagine it being a rolling ball. The ball has motion, and the basic movement is forward. But if we mark a spot on the ball and watch that spot, the spot is going backward half the time. With self and with friends, we need to keep the focus on the forward movement. We keep moving forward even while sometimes looking backward.

Like everything I do or learn, I discovered this rolling ball thing the hard way. It's never been too difficult for me to watch the growth process of a friend and to encourage him or her when it's seemed that there is repetition or reverting to old patterns—or stagnancy. But with myself, I got into trouble. It was then I learned about the backward look.

My whole life seemed to be messed up. Or, maybe I should say "messed down." Everything appeared to be on the downtrend, and I was worried. Spiritually, I felt out of touch with the Lord. Intellectually, I felt rusty because I was taking a couple classes and discovered that at middle age learning comes slower than it once did. Physically, I felt blah because I'd gained weight again and dreaded the process of getting it off. Emotionally, I felt angry at some situations in my life, and I thought I'd worked it out about anger (had even written about it!). Relationally, I felt separated and cut off from my friends. I wanted to withdraw and sit on my favorite end of the sofa.

Instead of withdrawing, though, I talked with my friends. When I shared that I was convinced I was going backward, Christy asked me why that made a difference. I answered that I felt afraid that she and the others in the group would not

love me and accept me if I went back to my old patterns.
Even as I said the words, they rang untrue.

And my friends' responses rang untrue, also. Only as I went
home that day and brooded about it did I see why: My
friends were feeding back to "unloved" and "unaccepted."
The falseness in this became apparent to me when I realized
that I no longer *felt* unloved and unaccepted as I once did. I
know now that I was on the spot on the ball that looks backward. But, then, not understanding the dynamics of how the
ball moved, I'd decided I *was* going backward. I had responded to the present situation with words from where I
used to be just because I was convinced of going backward.
In T.A. (transactional analysis) language, I was playing old
tapes. When I got to the bottom of the whole mess, I discovered that my main problem was the fear of going back because it implied failure—and focusing on the backward look.

The reason I, or any of us, become confused and focus on
the backward look is because there often is similarity in the
things we face now and the things of the past. If there were
not, we'd be in big trouble because nothing in our personhood
would tie together and have any continuity.

Take, for example, the anger in me: that it's there doesn't
mean I've gone back to where I was. There is a lot of
difference in being an angry person and being angry in a
specific situation. Now that I've pretty much worked the
anger out of my life as a whole, I still have the anger of
specific situations to deal with.

My mistake was in placing too much importance on the
backward look and not seeing its purpose at this point in my
total growth process. When, instead, I placed the emphasis on
the basic forward motion of my life, everything looked
different. I saw that all the things in my life that appeared to
be on the downtrend were, instead, a dormant state in my
personal growth. It was a resting time, a time to draw inward

a little and to re-examine and relax. I almost missed it because I was looking in the wrong direction.

Thus, focusing on the backward look instead of the basic forward motion of my process can slow my growth and cause me to miss the experience of it.

Focusing on the backward instead of the forward in a friend has an even more serious consequence: I may miss having that person for a friend—or, I will miss enjoying him as fully as possible.

Missing out happens in another way when we limit our acceptance to those who are the same as us.

Differences are part of life, and it is diversity that makes us unique individuals. To deny a friend his uniqueness is to keep him from being the person God created. Acceptance of differentness will expand possibilities for friendship.

If we consider Jesus' friends, we see that He did not choose friends by sameness. The disciples, Jesus' closest friends, were a motley bunch. There were plenty of individual quirks, personality traits and different beliefs among the twelve. No two people could have been more different than Matthew the tax collector (a traitor to his country), and Simon the Zealot (the superpatriot). Both men were far different from Jesus himself. Yet Jesus brought these two men together and made them his friends, and friends of each other.

Just so, today Jesus gives us the ability to reach out and make friends of those who are unlike us.

Probably the most difficult difference for us, as Christians, to accept, is people who have beliefs opposed to ours. For example, we are increasingly faced with persons involved in the human potential and Far-Eastern religious philosophies. We often cut those people out of our lives immediately because their concepts are strange to us. Most of us are skeptical, as we should be, about techniques such as meditation and fasting for purification of the body. Some of us simply cover our eyes and ears and run away from danger.

Certainly there is danger involved when these concepts are employed to put man in God's position. All through the scriptures I've run into verses warning that nothing is to take God's place of predominance in our thoughts and lives.

But for us as God's people to automatically cut off the people who believe in these different philosophies and techniques, means that we are eliminating a lot of people as potential friends.

Besides, if we listen, we might have something to learn from these people. I do think it's necessary to be cautious here. Sometimes thoughts and ideas can creep insidiously into our minds and draw us subtly away from God's truth. But I believe that Christ protects me from what is false or evil if I ask Him to. And so, in accepting someone with different beliefs and listening to that person to see if I can learn from her —I always pray that the Lord will shield me and be my teacher.

For example, when I attended some classes taught by a man who leans toward humanism, some of my friends criticized me. But I went to the classes, taking a Christian friend along so that I was not relying totally on my own judgment. We prayed before going into class to be protected, if necessary, from false "truth." And prayed daily for that protection during the times between classes. What I learned during that time was that some humanistic concepts and techniques can be beneficial to Christians as long as we rely on God's potential and not human potential.

Meditation, for example, doesn't have to be some strange phenomenon that includes chanting and mantras. Meditation has a place in Christian life. We can meditate on scripture, on the Lord and even about ways Christ is working in us. The humanists sometimes use their hands in meditation. And guess what? Hands in the prayer position! When the hands touch in this way, and all attention is focused for a few moments on the hands, the parts of the brain that control thinking and intuitive sense are able to relax. Our mind is ready to function at its best, and I think the Lord would enjoy getting our best now and then!

Fasting is mentioned quite often in the Bible, but many of us have never tried it. When I wanted to try fasting, I couldn't find one Christian friend who could tell me much about "how to." But in the "humanistic" class I attended, I learned much about fasting. For example, it's better for my body if I don't just get up one morning and quit eating. Instead, get into the fast slowly, over a period of two days, by eating only raw vegetables and juice the first day, and then only vegetable juice the second. Ending the fast slowly by the reverse of this is advisable. The middle days can be water only, but I've never been quite that brave! A caution, too: check with your doctor *before* fasting. Humanists fast to purify their bodies. I believe the Lord would have us fast because we can focus with greater clarity on the things of the Spirit when we set aside the physical for a time.

Maybe people with differing ideas are not as different as we think they are. The main difference is that they know only part of the truth because they don't know the Lord. Only we who do, can introduce them to Him. And one of the ways to do so is to say yes to them as persons; accept them as friends.

A second way we limit potential friends is by refusing to befriend those for whom we have no affinity or feeling of attraction.

There are times when a spark flies between us and another person, and it's easy to say yes to those people. But acceptance of people without regard to immediate affinity is a necessity if we are to ever have more than one or two friends. That's because the spark doesn't fly all that often.

If I were to befriend only the people to whom I am instantly attracted, I'd have very few friends. Even when I've felt that spark for someone, I've only once known for sure that she felt it too. So, maybe I'd only have one friend if I relied on instant affinity! Rather, for me—and I think for everyone—it's better to accept the other as a friend and let the feelings of attraction develop as they will. Affinities often come later, as friendship grows.

Another dynamic concerning acceptance is that it means seeing people as God does: holy. By this, I mean that He looks not to what is wrong with us, or what we look like from the outside, but to the inner potential for good.

For God it's settled. We are holy, potentially good, because Jesus made us that way the day He died on the Cross. We're already covered for the wrong things in our lives, and we belong to Him—if we believe.

For us humans, it's not so settled. Our concept of acceptance is based more on external appearances. That's not surprising, only human. Scripture tells us:

. . . for the Lord sees not as man sees; man looks on the outward appearance, but the Lord looks on the heart. (I Sam. 16:7, RSV)

This external focus actually hinders acceptance. For example, in myself: If I am in a flurry or confused or momentarily unhappy, I start thinking something is wrong with me. I'm unacceptable because I'm looking at the temporary responses to my situation. If I'm ill, I get frustrated because I think I must have done something wrong to cause that, and so forth. With others, if I base acceptance on some action or words that I don't approve, I'll always find some reason to put my friend in the "wrong" category, too. This makes for a very limited area of acceptance, if any at all.

Another way of looking to the outside and placing value there is in our human focus on success, performance, talent and material possessions. These things we value most often stand in the way of acceptance because we expect too much or more than what is possible. One of the most successful and talented women I know cannot accept herself unless she is performing and producing. And she has trouble accepting her friends who do not measure up to her standards of excellence. Others of us may measure by standards different from hers, but the truth is that all too often, we rely on these external barometers to decide whether or not a person is acceptable.

But how do we move from our viewpoint to God's and begin to see the inner potential for good in our friend?

Much of it is a matter of attitude. That makes it difficult because attitudes do not change readily.

Helpful to me in this area has been trying to visualize and brood upon God's love for us. I think about it and try to grasp the preciousness of His love. I read the first chapter of Ephesians over and over, because that helps me to perceive something of the depth of His love.

Sometimes it helps me to look at it from the reverse side, too. I think about my worst fault, the really negative thing that I'm embarrassed to share even with my best friends. At times, it's plural! Then I just dwell on how much God loves me in spite of that.

All this means God must have to look pretty hard sometimes to see the good in me. And it means I have to look hard to see the good in others. Sometimes the good is hidden very deep, under a bunch of other stuff. That means searching, even digging, for the good.

Once we have grasped onto the good, or even onto the potential for good in a friend, something wonderful happens. Somehow by recognizing goodness and saying yes to it, we draw it forth and make the good a reality in our friend's life. Over time, this recognition of the good makes it better. This calling forth of good, as we try to see our friend from God's viewpoint, is one of the most beautiful things that can happen in a friendship.

But it's not only beautiful. Seeing people as God does enables us to put acceptance into action in specific situations where we might otherwise find it difficult.

For one thing, it helps us not to ask others to change. To ask a friend to change will either delay or prohibit any change —even if that is something she needs very much. When we perceive that a friend has an area in her life that needs alteration, we need to respect her soul enough to allow her to do as she wishes about it. If a friend feels dominated or pushed, her response will be counterattack rather than change.

In Bible Study Fellowship as we studied the minor prophets, our lecturer constantly reminded us that we could not look at the people in the Old Testament from our perspective. The Cross changed the view. We can't expect them to have known what we know about God.

In a somewhat similar way, we cannot expect a friend to know what we know. We have a different vantage point. We need to respond to others from their perspective.

This can be put into practice in a way that helps the friend to make the changes in his life. When a friend shares a problem, it's best not to say everything we know or see about the problem. That might be too much all at once, or much as we hate to admit it, we might be misinterpreting the problem. Instead, it's better to respond to our friend with feedback that matches the place where he is working for change. This will help our friend move beyond that place and discover a direction to go.

Acceptance in action makes it possible for us to trust God for change or healing in a friend's life. We cannot do that for anyone. To attempt to do so is to be manipulative. Sometimes, though, it's difficult for us Christians to learn where our responsibility lies.

We get mixed up about our responsibility because we forget that it is God who does the healing. We start trying to take over His job. Whether physical pain or emotional change, we try to heal all the wounds of the past and the present—and prevent those of the future. Even the scar tissue left from healing annoys us and gives us fits because we look at it as remembered pain. But a doctor friend told me that from a medical point of view, scar tissue is good: It indicates that healing has taken place. Our scars, whether physical or emotional, should be worn as badges of honor, the signs of God's healing in our lives. When we leave the healing to God we no longer feel responsible to make changes of any kind for our friend. We instead, by acceptance, set the conditions for healing or change.

Setting the conditions for healing or change through acceptance isn't too difficult if a friend's need is one of the acceptable variety, such as minor behavior changes or physical illness. But some needs frighten us—like emotional illness.

Emotional needs frighten us because the person often engages in strange behavior or expresses strong negative emotions, the kind many of us were taught to repress. But we're all human enough and neurotic enough that we are able to recognize some of these strange things lurking around inside us, too. Being with a disturbed person makes us fear that we might act the same way. We want to draw back.

The other thing that may cause us to draw back is the fear of being hooked or manipulated. Sometimes disturbed persons are very manipulative. By playing psychological games they can put us into a place where they have control.

For example, the threat of suicide can sometimes be just a game to gain and keep attention. And, does it ever capture attention! When a woman kept calling me to "say good-bye," it took me four weeks to get the point that she was playing games with me. When we've been hooked a time or two like that, it's difficult *not* to draw back from those who suffer emotionally.

The instant we draw back, though, we prevent any possibility of helping. We're much like the disciples who were threatened by the possibility of danger to themselves when Jesus needed them. Instead of staying to help, they ran. We run even faster than they, sometimes, when we see someone who needs emotional support.

This was demonstrated at a conference I attended several years ago. During the meetings, it became quite obvious that a young girl there was severely depressed. From across the room I could see the looks on the faces of the people near her. I made a mental note to talk to her later. But just then we were asked to have a sharing time as part of the meeting. The girl began to talk, her words interspersed with deep, racking sobs. The whole crowd visibly stiffened—including the leaders. It made me wonder that no one near her was willing to reach out and touch her, hold her and accept her. I felt doubly guilty for myself: I knew what she needed, and was unwilling to "make a scene" by getting up and crossing a roomful of people to get to her. Later, I did go to speak to her, but I was too late. She'd already felt unaccepted.

I'm convinced that much emotional illness is more a mix-up in the communication process than an illness. Rather than say, "I need help, I can't cope anymore," a person engages in an attention-getting behavior, something that we label "crazy." Maybe those who are psychotic have gone too far and established irreversible patterns. I don't know. But I do think that there are many persons who can be helped if we recognize their need as an inability to communicate in a straight way.

Recognizing emotional needs as a communication mix-up

makes it possible to overcome our fear of such things and gives us a way to deal with the problems without becoming hooked ourselves. It enables us to see the needs from a different perspective and befriend a person when he or she perhaps needs it most. Sometimes only listening to someone at a time like this, without being shocked, will help that person to articulate what the underlying need is. He or she is able to find a way to straight communication. Sometimes that doesn't work. But if we offer our friendship when a person is needy emotionally, at least we've tried *something*.

One of the things about Jesus was that He befriended the people no one else wanted around. Tax collectors were hated. Lepers were sent out of town. That's just about the way emotional needs are looked upon by our society. But Jesus ate with tax collectors *and* sinners (Mark 2), and healed lepers (Mark 1). He also healed people with demons—probably those we'd call emotionally disturbed. He still does heal. If we can overcome our fear and say yes, be willing to be a friend, we may help set the conditions necessary for that person's healing.

But there is also a negative kind of condition we set in friendships, and it can be named "setups." In setups we precondition or have expectations, first, that there will be a friendship, and then, what it must be, or what must happen in a given encounter with a friend. Acceptance means learning to recognize when we are doing this—because it is sometimes very subtle—and then acting and responding in the friendship in a more natural way.

Most of us have difficulty determining the ways we engage in these setups. It's easier to see other people doing it to us! Probably the more we think we avoid preconditioning our friendships, the more out of touch we are with just how much we do expect.

For me, that's how it worked. I didn't think I had expectations of anyone until I could see it displayed right before my eyes. I was going to meet someone whom I felt was very important, a woman I'd admired and had wished to know. I daydreamed, imagined, anticipated. I decided I'd like this person, that she'd like me, and we'd be friends forever. I even ran back and forth through the conversation deciding what would be said and when. The daydreaming and anticipation are partly what makes a new friendship fun. But when the actual encounter comes, the daydreams are best left at home so that they don't grow into expectations. By the time I'd actually met my imagined bosom buddy, all my preconceptions of what it would be like were shattered. Where I'd decided there would be a friendship, one could not exist. The conversation was totally unlike that of my imagination, but it was the most straightforward communication I think I've ever had with anyone. I grew in the encounter when I acknowledged to myself the setup I'd made and then was able to give it up, without feeling rejected personally. And I learned that not everyone can or wants to be a friend. When I offer friendship to another, I should not expect programmed "results."

Perhaps the most difficult thing to learn about acceptance is the timing involved in the process. Some of us are like spiritual forerunners, out there urging our friends on, when the race is being run by those who can barely crawl. We become so enthusiastic about the race that we even get ahead of God some of the time.

Here we need to learn to slow down a little. Most helpful is remembering how long it takes to change even the smallest things in our own lives. That will help us to accept a friend's process when it looks slow.

Habits, for example, even when learned as an adult, take time and perseverance to change. A few years ago when I was first learning to do needlepoint, I somehow got mixed up and alternated stitches. I did the tent stitch one row and the half-cross stitch the next row. From the front on a small piece it didn't look too bad even so. But when I started a large wall-hanging, the lady at the needlepoint shop insisted that I'd have to choose one stitch or another. Sounds simple. But it took months before I could needlepoint and not have to concentrate on every single stitch.

Those habits learned as a child are even worse. I see it in little everyday things. For instance, I still fold towels the way my mother taught me, even though that means I have to refold them when I take them out of the closet to hang them on the towel bar. Not very important, but a bother.

More important habits are sometimes very deeply ingrained. One of mine is always being in a rush. I rush even when I'm going somewhere just for fun. One day I decided to take an afternoon off for lunch alone and really indulge myself. I drove the coast route to a favorite restaurant and decided to enjoy the time thoroughly. Instead, I found myself rushing, trying to get there by a certain time. Halfway there, I realized that I had not even noticed the beauty of the ocean beside the road. This experience did not change my habit of rushing. It just began the process.

Friendship means learning to accept each other where we are in the process. Sometimes it's difficult to accept even our own process, let alone that of a friend. Learning about our own timing can give us new acceptance for a friend's process.

A friend, whom I will call Millie, had been struggling with rebellion for a long time. The rebellion focused itself on relationships with other people, self-indulgence and lack of discipline, and, worst of all, against God. Millie had tried everything she knew to overcome the problem with her own resources. Increasingly, she found herself lying awake at night, praying, asking God to help her change, searching for a solution. Each morning when she awoke, the problem was still there.

Finally, Millie began, out of desperation, to trust that Christ was "in the process" with her, though she could not see an apparent change. She knew she had to believe that in His own time, He would bring her through it, and she was incapable of doing it herself. Millie accepted God's timetable and crawled along with it, for however long that might be. A few months later, she picked a book off the library shelf simply because it looked interesting.

The book was more than interesting. It put Millie in touch with the guilt that caused her rebellion. She recalled specific incidences and dialogued with her memories. She realized that she had, in her inner mind, someone who constantly pointed the finger, telling her not to do many of the things she did. Because of her guilt, even a simple thing like relaxing became a waste of time, caused anxiety, then rebellion which led to relaxing so much that she lost discipline. Her rebellion against guilt caused her to rebel also against anyone she suspected of coercing her. She went on, through all the many facets of the problem, and discovered as she did that it was a cycle, each part feeding on the other: guilt, rebellion, anxiety, more guilt and so on.

Finally, Millie realized that being a Christian had not eased, but intensified, her guilt feelings. She realized that she looked upon God as a Finger-pointing Someone who made her do what He demanded. As she prayed to be released from her guilt and rebellion cycle through whatever was God's will, Millie at last found the answer. Deep inside, she knew for certain that God was not the finger pointer she'd imagined. She no longer must stand before Him as a guilty and rebellious little girl. This broke the entire cycle apart, and Millie is learning not to live out of rebellion.

Though the final discovery happened in a breakthrough manner, Millie knew that God had been preparing her step-by-step along the way to the solution. Only by being willing

to trust His timing, did she find the acceptance to live out the
process.

Since then, Millie told me, it's been easier to accept the
process in her friends. She knows they're moving one step at a
time, and someday they'll finish the race. She accepts the timing involved and encourages her friends without insisting that
they move faster.

But what about the times, when no matter how hard we try,
we still have trouble accepting something about a friend—or a
friend's slow progress, or his tendency to revert to old patterns, like Pige's circle-turning, is driving us crazy?

Here, the only thing we can do is to start trusting God, not
only for our lack of acceptance, but for His work in our
friend's life. The way things look to us may not be so important.

For example, in the story of the blind man (John 9), the
way things looked to the Pharisees and even to the disciples
was that the man was blind because of sin. This made acceptance of the man and even of his healing, impossible. They
kept looking for somebody or something to blame. Whose
fault was it? But, Jesus saw it all in another way: God's work.
The rest of it, no matter how it looked, was unimportant.

Seeing God's work, or if we can't *see* it, just trusting that He
*is* there working, for no other reason than He's *said* He will be
—helps us to put our unacceptable-looking friend into perspective and to rejoice for the work that is going on.

A story in Ezra teaches us something about *when* to rejoice.
The Israelites had just returned to Jerusalem after captivity,
and the foundation of the Temple had been laid. The work
wasn't anywhere near done. Just begun. But:

. . . the priests in their vestments came forward with trumpets,
and the Levites . . . with cymbals, to praise the Lord, according to

the directions of David king of Israel; and they sang responsively, praising and giving thanks to the Lord . . . (Ezra 3:10–11, RSV.)

We, too, need to rejoice for the work that is going on: not for the finished work, but for the present work that the Lord is doing in our friend's life.

Rejoicing before the work is finished makes it possible to say the final word of acceptance: *Yes!*

# SIX

## Honesty:
## No Spiritual Lollipops

She called about 10 P.M. one weekend evening just as I'd settled into my favorite corner of the sofa with a good book.

Until I discovered the reason for her call, I was quite flat-
tered that someone from so far away had heard of me. She'd
seen my first book, read the title, and phoned. She hadn't
bothered to read the book! Her call really frightened me. She
intended to "go to sleep tonight and just not wake up in the
morning." Her slurred voice convinced me that she might be
serious.

After listening to her for two hours, I made her promise to
write to me in the morning. I felt relieved, and was exhausted
enough to sleep well that night.

The calls came rapidly after that. Sometimes two a day, or a
day or two apart. She always phoned at inconvenient hours
like dinner time, late evening unwinding time, or even after
I'd gone to bed. I don't know when she slept—many of the
calls were at three or four in the morning her time.

Always, she was lonely. Once, she'd run away from home.
Maybe she'd come to see me. She thought she might kill herself anyway, especially if I didn't have time to listen. I gave

her the number of the suicide hotline in her city, and encouraged her to call the mental health clinic. She went to a counselor there once and decided she "could not relate to that person."

She also wrote, not only as I'd suggested the first night, but oodles of long disturbed letters. For the first time in my life I did not look forward to the arrival of the mail. I began to put the letters in a drawer, unopened.

But how could I not read her letters, or not listen to her, much less tell her that she was disturbing my life? My kids started referring to her as my "problem lady," and they listened to my end of the "conversation" with long, solemn looks on their faces.

Increasingly, I knew that this woman needed a lot more help than a sympathetic ear in California could give. So, I gathered my courage and suggested, rather strongly, that she go to a psychologist for therapy. To my surprise, she went.

I thought my troubles were ended. Instead, they continued and worsened.

She called to tell me everything she'd told the psychologist. Then she told me the things she could not tell the psychologist—the things she "could never discuss with a man."

I was at wits' end. I felt totally helpless because she refused to consider my suggestions. Yet I felt responsible to keep her alive. Each time the phone rang, I felt my "fight and flight" button go off and the adrenalin flowing—just at a time when I was trying to keep stress at low key. I had been having intermittently high blood pressure and wanted to learn to keep it low without taking medication. So, not only could I not help her, but was going to need help myself to keep my health if I didn't do something *about* her, and soon.

But what could I do? Didn't being a friend mean "being nice" and just listening? She'd feel rejected if I asked her not to call. Was I truly responsible if she *did* take her life? What did it mean to extend Christ's love to a person like her? What about the fact that I'd had no training in counseling, and here I was, a neophyte, naïvely running a "counsel by phone" service? The more questions I asked myself, the deeper my predicament became. I was in over my head, emotionally involved, and didn't have any idea what it meant to love or be a friend in this kind of situation.

With the help of two friends who have doctorates in psychology, I was able to sort things out and to see that by being nice, I was actually *increasing* this woman's problems. Her long-distance phone calls added up to a staggering figure, and she already had financial troubles. By listening to the things she would not share with her psychologist, I was interfering with the therapy and decreasing the possibility that she'd open up to him totally. And by allowing her to manipulate me into feeling responsible for her life, I was nourishing her illness rather than helping to make her well.

Seeing the situation from this perspective, I realized that to *really* love her was to be totally straight with her and ask her not to call again. This would give her the freedom to move beyond her illness. Being honest with her was one of the most difficult things I've done in my life.

This situation with my "problem lady" was extreme, but it taught me the importance of honesty in friendship, and jolted me out of my "spiritual" misunderstandings about what it means to love one another as Christ commanded. Like many Christians, I'd always thought of love only as being nice. Smile, even if I have to grit my teeth to do it.

At the very least, this misconception puts my personal integrity on almost the zero level and means I will probably spend a lot of time gritting my teeth.

To the friend who is the recipient of my niceness, I may just as well be giving a spiritual lollipop when what he or she needs is a balanced diet. Just as a diet based on sugar will destroy our bodies, spiritual lollipops will destroy and prevent real friendship.

True, being nice and handing out spiritual lollipops makes people feel good, at least temporarily. It often leaves them with the impression that we are meeting their needs, when in reality we may be holding them back or preventing them from having their real needs met.

Honesty is not easy, and it makes us uncomfortable. But it's a good back-door strategy, and it really gets us beyond the lollipops and good feelings and inside each other's lives.

Unfortunately, there's no recipe for honesty—or any printed daily menus to follow. It's mostly a matter of cutting down on the sugar (we still need *some* niceness and good feelings!) and trying to balance the ingredients. With no rules to follow, there's a lot of decision making to do.

First, we must decide whether or not we should be honest.

I think it's necessary to have a certain degree of friendship before honesty is possible. Honesty has more to do with keeping friends than making friends. There has to be a basic underlying acceptance of our friend as a person. Honesty becomes a kind of completion step to acceptance, urging our friend more fully into his or her forward process.

In deciding whether to be honest with a friend, it's necessary to ask a few questions. For example: My friend has hurt my feelings; I've felt ignored and unimportant to her. Should I be honest, and confront her with my feelings, or not say anything? A helpful question is to ask myself if I'd want to know when I'd hurt my friend's feelings that way. Probably I would if I really cared about her.

Next in deciding whether to be honest is clarifying the reason for my honesty. It is for my good only? Or is it for the good of my friend, too, and the ultimate good of the friendship? It's important that my basic loyalty is to the friendship, and *not* to proving myself right.

If I see my friend engaging in destructive behavior, I only encourage that behavior if I am not willing to challenge it. Do I care enough about my friend to risk telling her that the way she's acting is hurting our friendship?

When there is a conflict between my friend and me, I am most comfortable covering it up and pretending it's not there. Or when the conflict is severe, I am tempted to run. But covering it up prevents intimacy with my friend, and running terminates the friendship. Honesty provides continuity through conflict. Disagreements don't divide, but refusal to handle them honestly *does*.

Christy told me about her struggle in learning to handle conflict.

She discovered that she resisted conflict with her friends; her concept of friendship was one of avoidance. She believed that if a friendship was worth keeping, it was necessary to simply accept annoyances and hurtful situations as part of the deal. For this reason she resisted the signs that indicated there was conflict in some of her friendships—until a friend honestly confronted her.

"It was difficult," Christy recalls. "I almost felt as if she'd broken the rules of the game—the ways I thought a friendship operated. She was showing me things about myself I didn't like. I couldn't handle it all at once. I had to go home and write pages in my journal before I could discern which of the things she said were legitimate and which were not. By that, I mean that I didn't have to buy the whole thing. I had a choice to decide what was really true about me. It helped me during the confrontation that I was in touch with my own feelings. Because I didn't have any anger or anything that was submerged, I didn't need to strike out and perhaps cause a free-for-all. Basically, her honest sharing changed my concept about friendship and what it can be. Confrontation removes barriers that keep relationships from deepening, thus extending the possibilities for friendship."

The conflict in this friendship had built up for a long time. There was a deep residue of hurt in the other person, and Christy believes that made the confrontation more difficult for both of them. She now feels that the sooner the conflict is dealt with, the better. It saves putting everything that's said into the framework of hurt and eliminates the probability of reading implications into the words that aren't there.

In a group situation, for example, Christy was confronted honestly by a new friend. The conflict was dealt with immediately. Here is Christy's account from her journal about the differences in the two situations:

With_____, I ignored the conflict until it burst out of her. By then she had so much hurt and emotion stored up that she really let me have it. There were side issues, past emotions and lots of junk surrounding the original issue.

With_____, it was clean: We disagreed on an issue, we confronted each other without any side issues or past emotions, we listed the alternatives and through the group decided on an acceptable compromise, and there was reconciliation right then.

Through these experiences, Christy has come to believe that conflict may actually be creative. Instead of avoiding it, she now encourages bringing it to the surface where it can be dealt with.

In deciding whether to be honest, it's also helpful to look at Jesus to see what is really Christian. Jesus was incredibly honest. He didn't grit his teeth and smile at the Pharisees. He challenged them often about their preference for tradition rather than for people.

Jesus also challenged destructive behavior. For example, in John 5, Jesus saw through the sick man at the pool and asked if he really wanted to be healed. The man was so caught up in his destructive behavior of blaming others for his continued illness that he could not even give Jesus a direct answer. Instead, he listed his excuses for staying sick. Jesus cut right through the man's indirectness, ignored the excuses, and told the man to get up and walk.

And when it comes to conflict, Jesus gave us quite specific instructions in Matthew 5:23-24 (RSV):

So if you are offering your gift at the altar, and there remember that your brother has something against you, leave your gift there before the altar and go; first be reconciled to your brother, and then come and offer your gift.

That calls for honesty!

Once we've decided that we must be honest with our friend, we must then decide *when* to be honest.

The "roots" of the problem have something to do with the when. It's necessary to clarify exactly what the problem is. Maybe there is something in a friend's behavior that really drives me crazy. Well, it could be *my* problem—maybe I need to be honest with myself!

A good way to check this out is with a trusted mutual friend. A friend, not friends! It's important that this doesn't become a gossip session, and talking to someone, not everyone, keeps that from happening.

If the mutual friend perceives the problem to be similar to what I have discovered, and has perhaps been offended by the same behavior in our mutual friend, then I can be fairly sure that I have not manufactured the problem myself, and it might be the right time for an honest confrontation.

Concern for a friend's situation is an absolute necessity for the when. Sometimes this just requires common sense. If our friend has a houseful of company or a sick child, we can be pretty certain that now is not when! But sometimes it really is difficult to tell if the timing is right. Our friend may be loaded down with things we cannot see.

For example, a few months ago, one of my friends had hurt my feelings. She'd been distant, almost cool, and I did not understand why. The only time she phoned me or communicated in any way was when she wanted me to do something for her. She's a good friend, so I didn't have to think much about the whether—I knew she'd want to know. I'd also talked the problem through with a mutual friend and knew this coolness on the part of my friend was really coming from her and not from me. I was ready to be honest until I realized that the when was wrong. Two or three other people had already confronted her about this and other problems. Her marriage was very strained. She was being bombarded with honesty. No wonder she seemed preoccupied and distant. For me to have gone to her at that time would have been more honesty than necessary, *and* cruel. Too many confrontations all at once make it feel like a "they got me" day to someone already loaded down. At times like this, we need to understand our friend's predicament and put the lid on our honesty, at least for the present.

The third kind of decision making about honesty concerns how. This has to do with communication.

Communications can mean double-trouble. They can become garbled on either side—our form of speech can be unclear or our friend's hearing can be distorted. We can't do very much about the distortions in a friend's hearing process. But we *can* make certain that the message we send is clear and free from garble.

The words we speak should reflect our true position and say what we mean. They should be specific.

The best way of learning to do this is to become aware of the ways our words fall short of saying what we really mean.

It's easiest for me to see this with my kids because they can be so straight. When they want to be! They listen to my semi-garbled communications and understand perfectly well what I mean to say. But they love to play a little game with me: "But, Mo-o-om, you *said* to do that." When they were little, "that" meant putting a swimsuit on the cement to dry instead of hanging it over the line or a chair—because I'd said to put the suit *on* the patio to dry. Now that they're older and have perfected the game a bit, I'm learning to be more and more specific. The possibilities of being "misinterpreted" could be more serious than just a dirty swimsuit!

My friend Elsie learned about specifics, too, in a really humorous way. The family was moving to the country, and on a Sunday drive in the area where their new house was being built they'd found a cow skull. Elsie thought it a perfect decoration for her future country garden, so she put it in the car. Monday morning, when Davy was looking for something to do, Elsie suggested that he "wash that cow skull in the car." He did wash it—right in the car! The waterlogged car wasn't a bit funny then, but Elsie and I have had a lot of good laughs over it since. And it taught us to be more careful and specific about what we say in all situations.

A second way to ungarble communications we send is to stay in touch with our inner being enough that the verbal and the non-verbal are saying the same thing. Otherwise we risk sending double messages, with the non-verbal saying just the opposite of our words. Even if the friend who is listening doesn't fully understand the reason for the confusion, he or she may not believe the verbal message just because something rings untrue.

These double messages have the added effect of putting a friend in a double bind. Verbally, I might say something like this, "What do you think of this casserole? It's a new recipe." Non-verbally, especially if I've had a difficult day and need a little praise, I might be saying, "You'd better like it or else!

I've worked all day cooking it!" My friend in that situation probably doesn't know what to say if the casserole is *not* tasty. If she answers the non-verbal and says it's a great casserole, when *I* know it's lousy, I feel dissatisfied. And if she honestly tells me she dislikes it, even though I know it's not good, I might just think my friend is being overly critical—she wouldn't have liked anything I'd done today. Either way, my friend's answer is displeasing.

With things like the casserole, it's simple enough to see how we send double messages. In friendships, it takes a bit more detective work.

Only a few days ago I watched closely as a friend spoke. Verbally she was saying she felt okay about all that had been said that day by some other people. But I suspected she had been hurt by some of the words, so I looked specifically for that hurt. It was so subtle I would have missed it if I were not looking. But it was there, in a smile that almost bordered on tears. My friend didn't recognize that she was hurt, either. Because she had not looked inside, she had no idea that her verbal message did not agree with the non-verbal.

Thus, if we are to send pure and undistorted communications, we must constantly strive to keep the words we speak in line with inner thoughts and feelings. Honesty is impossible if we don't.

Another part of the how of honest communication is gentleness. An attitude of concern for our friend's feelings is crucial. Quickly spoken and unthoughtful words can turn best intentions into a destructive force. And the destruction done is to the friendship.

The book of James has much to say about the tongue and about being slow to speak. A time spent meditating and praying before confronting a friend in honesty will help in the choice of the words, the tone of voice and the extent of the communication. It might be better to say only a little at a time rather than all at once.

How we communicate is important in still another way. When approaching a friend it's best to do so from the stand-point of how *I* am. What I feel, what I think, what I want, what I need.

This is difficult for a lot of us, who, as Christians, think we should always be thinking about what the other person needs or wants, thinks or feels. Since childhood, we've learned to hide the fact that we have needs and wants. As a result, when we try to communicate to a friend, it often comes off as an accusation: what a friend has done wrong, instead of what I want or feel.

For example, I can accuse my friend, "Why don't you ever spend more time with me?" But I can better say it from where I am, and avoid blaming my friend, "I'd like to have more time with you. Could we schedule a lunch date next week?"

Refusing to say where I am leads not only to accusations, but also to little white lies. It's considered socially acceptable to say to my friend, "Sorry, I can't come to your dinner party. I'm busy that night." And, then, sit home. How much better to say, "I really need some time alone to get some reading done. I'd better stay home. But thank you for wanting me."

All this does not mean ignoring our friend's wants and needs, or expecting to have everything our way. It's important to listen to and respond to the needs of our friend, and if those needs clash with ours, compromise. I just mean that honest expression of how I am is the thoughtful way to communicate.

How to communicate might mean learning more or brush-ing up on communication skills. Lately, for instance, I'm learning that I'm weak on verbal skills, or at least on using the ones I know. If I wrote out everything I ever said, there wouldn't be much problem. That gives me time to think. But verbal skills mean quick responses, and I am slow verbally. So, I'm planning to take a course to improve.

Still another decision: being honest with a friend has some potential for difficulties. It's necessary to decide what to do about any difficulty that might arise.

One possibility is resistance on the part of our friend. Sometimes it seems a friend just is not hearing what we've said. This calls for persistence.

In one situation, for example, I decided to be honest with a friend about how I was reacting to her attitude toward me. It was terribly difficult to do this in the first place. It had taken me weeks to decide whether or not to do it, and then weeks more to decide when and how. Finally, the time seemed right, and trying my best, shaking all over, I talked to my friend about the problem. She brushed me off, as if she hadn't heard a word I'd said. I had to begin all over and go through the whole communication again. Shaking worse the second time! I'm still not certain that my friend heard me.

But I'm persisting. It's good to remember that a troublesome situation is not often resolved at one particular point in time. Sometimes our communications need to be more of the on-going kind, gently persistent, until our friend hears.

Sometimes a friend will respond to our honesty with anger. Then it's necessary to learn not to be defensive. Our defensiveness keeps us from dealing with a friend's feelings and might even cause us to reciprocate with anger. Marshall Bryant Hodge explains this:

When we see the anger of another toward us as primarily an attempt to hurt us rather than an attempt to communicate feelings, and when we then reciprocate by attempting to hurt the other rather than primarily expressing our feelings, it seems unlikely that we can achieve any creative experience. We are most likely to fly off onto a tangent of accusation and probing at weak points in the other person's defenses where they can be hurt the most.[1]

Thus, when a friend responds to our honest sharing with anger, we need to choose not to yell and scream in return. It takes a lot of practice to do this—to sit and listen to a friend's angry words. But it's easier if our motives have been right from the beginning, when deciding whether to be honest. If our main concern in being honest then was for the good of the friendship, and not to prove that we're right, then it will be easier to opt for a soft response to the anger, without defensiveness.

The other side of anger is our own frustration when faced with someone's behavior, or even *dis*honesty. There is no place for venting angry feelings in being honest. This might be one of the hardest of the difficulties to work out. Especially when it might be justified to pound on the other person a bit!

Situations with repairmen have been most helpful to me in teaching me how to handle frustration without pounding on the other person. I try to apply what I'm learning in these situations to the times I have to deal with frustration concerning a friend.

Probably the most important thing I've learned in dealing with repairmen is to separate the situation from the person. Otherwise my frustration becomes so intense that I am overwhelmed by it—and then I just sputter.

When our TV lost its picture, I didn't really care. But the rest of the family did—so we took it in for repair. When I went to pick up the set, I discovered that in addition to soldering the broken circuits as needed, the repairman had somehow burned a hole in the center of the screen. Then the person at the pickup desk tried to tell me the hole had been burned when the picture first went out. Well, I would have had to be blind not to have seen it then. I just felt very deeply that the repair-shop people were being dishonest with me, and that I needed to firmly insist that something be done to correct the situation. For once I was able not to sputter at the person manning the pickup desk. He, personally, probably had nothing to do with it. This separation of the person from the problem enabled me to calmly and firmly insist that I be permitted to speak with the store manager. When I explained the whole situation to him, he arranged to have the picture tube replaced, free of charge. I'm certain we'd be staring at a hole in the middle of the picture tube today if I had allowed my frustration to rule my responses—as I have done before, and since!

Still another possible difficulty involved in being honest with a friend is guilt. Even when we've handled the entire process to the very best of our ability, guilt sometimes attacks.

A friend told me that this happened to her. She'd had an on-going problem with another woman. My friend is a really nice person, who has been taught since childhood that one *never* talks about a problem like this. Yet she really felt used and clutched upon in this particular friendship, and knew that if it were to continue she'd have to honestly talk to her friend. She handled it well, and over time managed to communicate what she was feeling—even though the process made her very nervous. But then, once it all worked out and was settled, my friend felt extremely guilty. All her early teachings about "being nice" piled up, resulting in tons of guilt. My friend had to decide all over again that her honest confrontation of this friend had been the best solution to the problem—and then choose not to feel guilty.

All this deciding about whether, when and how—along with working out the difficulties involved—might cause us to wonder if honesty in friendship is worth the effort.

Wouldn't it be easier just to go on being nice, handing out spiritual lollipops, and making people feel good?

Well, yes, it would be easier. But the result will be very superficial friendships, and short-term friends. Honesty, instead, provides for intimate and lasting friendship—gets us into a friend's life, and lets our friend inside ours. The friendship deepens.

Honesty like this leads us to a new concept of friendship: joint ownership.

Karl Olsson wrote about joint ownership in the October 1976 issue of *Faith/at/Work* magazine. Although Karl was speaking in terms of all types of relationships, I believe what he had to say applies even more specifically to friendship.

In the article, Karl included a sketch of two circles, each representing the potential self of the two persons involved. Inside each circle, a jagged smaller area indicated the actual self. Between each actual self was a bridge—representing the relationship between two people. Karl pointed out that this bridge is jointly owned by the two people. The necessary repairs and maintenance are a mutual responsibility.

If the friendship is owned by the two of us, that puts a different picture on being friends than what many of us have had in the past. Because we are Christian, some of us have felt we had total responsibility for maintaining the friendship. We are out there repairing the bridge and painting the lines down the middle and checking to see if the supports are secure—all alone. This is particularly true in dealing with non-Christian friends. Trying to live up to our "standards" of Christian behavior, we have felt driven to maintain and save a friendship at whatever the cost to ourselves. Which may be the very thing that keeps a given friendship from developing to its full potential.

A friend whom I will call Jody learned about joint ownership of the friendship bridge through a very difficult experience.

Jody had had a fairly good friendship for years with another woman about her same age. They just seemed to hit it off from the time they met at a dinner party given by a mutual friend. They had coffee together often, met for lunch, shopped together. The only thing that was a problem for Jody was that her friend had a quick flaring temper. Jody had seen the temper in action a couple times, and she felt she had to tread pretty carefully to avoid having it lashed out at her.

Finally, the friend's temper *was* lashed out against Jody. The worst part was that Jody had not done anything to earn her friend's anger. Because their husbands had had a disagreement, Jody's friend attacked her. Vicious accusations were flung at Jody, and she was dumbfounded. The friend declared that she did not want to continue being friends, period.

Because she cared deeply about preserving the friendship, Jody's first reaction was that she must save it, no matter what. She felt she must be the reconciler and patch things up. But as she thought about ways she could do that, the only idea which came to her mind was that she could go and apologize.

Apologize? For what? Jody saw clearly that this was not her problem. To apologize for something she had not done, just to save the friendship, was senseless. It turned her into a spineless, apologetic person who had to crawl back to her friend. Jody realized this was not the answer. She'd have to think of something else.

The something else Jody discovered was that being friends requires the efforts of two people. It was not her total responsibility to keep the friendship going. She began to understand her responsibility in a new way. This meant two things:

First, Jody realized that she could not allow her friend to dump the problem on her. It was necessary to allow the friend to own the problem. This called for an honest confrontation.

Her voice trembling, Jody telephoned her friend and invited her to meet for a talk. Then Jody gently, but firmly, said that she could not accept the responsibility for the broken friendship. To her surprise, Jody's friend did admit she had a problem with her temper and that it had gotten her into trouble many times.

Secondly, Jody understood her role as a reconciler to be vastly different than being spineless and apologetic. She realized that as the Christian member of the friendship, she was responsible to be the *initiator* of the reconciliation. But once she had taken the first step, she needed to wait for the other person to respond. And so, Jody's honesty included sharing the desire to continue being friends.

Unfortunately, Jody's friend was not ready to be reconciled. But Jody had learned that she could not force peace on anyone. In giving her friend the freedom to respond to the request for reconciliation, Jody also found freedom for herself. She could let go of feelings of being responsible for the friendship and allow it to be jointly owned.

Months later, the two friends *were* reconciled, and Jody found her own life changed by the experience. She discovered a new kind of humility in waiting for the friend to respond. Because she had always been the one to patch up the friendship, Jody had felt some pride in her ability to do so. Now, when she had to sit back and wait for her friend to take a step, Jody had to be the *recipient* in reconciliation. Because she had no power to change the situation other than making the initial step, Jody had to depend on Christ's power working in the broken friendship. Learning to be the recipient of reconciliation dashed her pride, but the friendship was restored.

One more thing about honesty: Part of the process is learning to be the recipient of honest communications. We need to be prepared to get back what we give out. This simply requires openness and receptivity—the desire to know our friend more intimately. It may sound simple, but will take some practice to make it happen. Just trying again when we have not been open will help us to be better recipients. It isn't automatic or easy.

Honesty is not easy from either side, whether we are giving or receiving. It takes a lot of effort. But deciding to go beyond the spiritual lollipop stage of superficial friendship makes honesty possible, even if it never becomes easy.

And as for the effort: deepening, enduring friendships are worth it!

# SEVEN

## Forgiveness: Disposing of the Mental Garbage

Friday is trash day at our house.

All week, every day, Sharon carries the waste paper basket outside and dumps the assorted discarded Kleenex, empty milk cartons and such into the large trash can. Then Steve pulls the big cans out to the curb early Friday morning. Next, the city collection crew roars down our street in a big growling truck and carries all our garbage to the dump. More politely, in San Diego, called the city landfill.

I'd be in a real mess if it weren't for those trash trucks coming by. I make a sincere effort to get all the garbage out of the corners of the house before the truck arrives. And on the rare occasions when Steve forgets to put the cans out front before he goes to school, *I* drag them out—even though they're much too heavy and getting them there ruins my back for days.

Trash day is important to me because without it, in a matter of weeks, I'd be up to my neck, inundated with the bit-by-bit accumulation of garbage. It would be impossible to function properly.

Neither can I nor any of us function with an accumulation of mental garbage. But we often try to do so by refusing to forgive our friends when they hurt us in some way. Not only do we store up and accumulate all the little hurts and frustrations —and the big ones, too—we go still further. We go through this mental garbage and rehash it, re-examine it, and try to figure out ways to get even.

This storing of the mental garbage caused by lack of forgiveness prevents friendship. Forgiveness is a critical part of back-door strategy: Unless we forgive, we will have no friends. The inevitable clashes that occur would make everyone a permanent enemy. As Eileen Guder says:

Everyone you know will be your enemy at some time—when he hurts you, or slights you, or takes sides again you. . . . Retaliation is fatal, for it deepens the enmity; wrong has been answered with wrong, and there is no end to that dreary road. Someone, somewhere along the line, has to reverse the process, has to do the painful but necessary deed of offering forgiveness . . .[1]

You and I, of course, are the "someones" who must reverse that process *if* we're serious about this business of making and keeping friends.

And, it *is* a painful deed. Sometimes forgiveness seems impossible. This is because we *choose* anger—which automatically blocks our ability to forgive.

A friend who lives in another state told me how she chose anger over forgiveness—even though she thought she *wanted* to forgive. Debbie's clash was with her pastor, whom she really wanted to befriend. (I've changed both Debbie's name and that of the pastor.)

A deeply committed Christian, Debbie has always been active in her church. Because of this and the smallness of her church, Debbie had had a close and satisfying friendship with her pastor for many years. When he retired due to illness, Debbie missed him, but looked forward with great anticipation to the arrival of a new pastor—and the making of a new friend.

Because she was Sunday school Superintendent, Debbie went to visit Reverend Worth soon after his arrival. She told him the details: what curriculum was being used, about the teachers, the basic approach to the teaching. Then Debbie asked if he, as pastor, would like any changes made. He assured her that she was doing a great job, and it would save him a lot of work if she'd just continue doing things as always. Debbie left feeling good about Reverend Worth's ready acceptance of her program—and very warmed by his pleasant and friendly response to her as a person.

Just a few months later, Debbie began to hear rumors and rumblings. It seemed that Reverend Worth had told several people that he was unhappy about the way Debbie had been running the Sunday school. A number of people had come to Debbie saying the pastor was unhappy. At first Debbie brushed these rumors aside as being meaningless—or maybe just gossip. During the months since they'd met, Debbie and Reverend Worth had deepened their friendship, and so she felt certain that he'd tell *her* if there were a problem.

But as the rumors continued, Debbie went to talk to the pastor, specifically about the Sunday school program. Was he happy with the work she'd done as Superintendent? Did he want any changes made, now that he'd been here for a while? Reverend Worth assured her that he was very pleased, affirmed her and even thanked her for the work she was doing. Again, Debbie left warmed and happy about her new pastor friend.

Still the rumblings continued, and Debbie became confused. When two of Debbie's teachers came to her and said that Reverend Worth wished she would change the curriculum, Debbie was dumbfounded. She no longer could view the comments she'd heard as meaningless and empty gossip.

"I felt he was refusing to be honest with me—telling me one thing, and saying something else to other people," Debbie remembers. "This meant he did not have any respect for me as a person. It was degrading to me, and to our friendship. Worse yet, he was my pastor. How could I trust my spiritual well-being to such a two-faced person?"

When Debbie went, after much thought and prayer, to honestly share her confusion and hurt feelings with Reverend Worth, one of her teachers who was also a friend, went along. Because he was a pastor, both women expected that he would be glad to work toward reconciliation in the matter. But they were surprised. Debbie says:

"It was really maddening that he would not communicate. We went there with the idea of straightening out the friendship. But it only seemed to make things worse. Reverend Worth would not even listen to me—he just kept interrupting to defend himself. He actually said I was to blame for the whole thing. I just kept feeling: It's no use. He is too pigheaded. He has hurt me, and now probably I've hurt him, too."

Debbie was crushed. When she left Reverend Worth, she was in tears, and she drove home howling all the way. But once she'd gone beyond the original shock, Debbie saw that she really hadn't been to blame for the disruption in the friendship. When she thought about the things Reverend Worth had said in defense of himself, she realized that he had a terrible problem with communication. Because he was so concerned with the happiness of his congregation, he didn't want to "rock anyone's boat." He simply agreed with what everyone said—even though quite often that meant he was agreeing with opposite opinions.

The ugly rumors about the Sunday school curriculum had begun in this way. To Debbie, Reverend Worth said he was pleased. To one of her teachers, who didn't like the curricu-

lum, he said, "Perhaps it can be changed." His double messages backfired on him when people in the congregation tried
to work together to carry out his opposite "desires." Nobody
knew what he *really* wanted, because he hadn't communicated
to them honestly.

With this knowledge, Debbie decided she would just have
to put her hurt feelings aside and forgive. But she found herself terribly angry and not *able* to forgive.

"It was on my mind some part of every day," Debbie recalls. "I kept telling myself that Reverend Worth is only a
man, just like the rest of us humans, imperfect. I had seen his
weakness, and part of me did not want to tear him apart for
it. But I had a real block in being able to forgive, because I
expected him, as pastor, to have more Christian maturity than
I. I was furious that he did not. And it made me more angry
that he did not make a move toward reconciliation and say he
was sorry. I started to hate him because I knew he was ugly
underneath the smile he always wore. And he kept acting as if
we still were friends—as if nothing were wrong. One morning
when he walked up behind me before church, and patted me
on the shoulder, I actually jumped. I did not want him to
touch me. Finally, I started feeling hostile about my whole
church and felt that I wanted to sabotage it or get even in
some way. If I left, they wouldn't have a Sunday school Superintendent, and that would be delicious retaliation. The
only thing that stopped me from leaving was that I kept remembering that it's Christ's church, and not Reverend
Worth's, or mine."

Debbie's choice to be angry and her nourishment of that
anger blocked her ability to forgive Reverend Worth—even
though she didn't *consciously* choose to be angry.

Probably the choice to be angry rather than forgive is made
subconsciously by most of us. For this reason, it is necessary
to identify and sort out some of the reasons we choose anger.

For one thing, as Frederick Buechner points out, anger is fun:

Of the Seven Deadly Sins, anger is possibly the most fun. To lick your wounds, to smack your lips over grievances long past, to roll over your tongue the prospect of bitter confrontations still to come, to savor to the last toothsome morsel both the pain you are given and the pain you are giving back—in many ways it is a feast fit for a king.

And, then, the consequences of unforgiveness:

The chief drawback is that what you are wolfing down is yourself. The skeleton at the feast is you.[2]

One of the other reasons we choose anger is that forgiveness is just not a part of our basic human nature. To forgive requires us to take a step beyond the inner desire to cling to a hateful attitude, making anger seem justified.

Just a few days ago, I spoke to a friend and told her I was beginning this chapter on forgiveness, and shared with her some of my ideas and ideals. My friend's response reflected the human nature to opt for anger:

"Good heavens, Jan, what are you trying to do? Become a perfect person? You're always beating yourself, taking the blame. Why do you even want to forgive someone who did *that* to you? You have a *right* to be angry."

Well, maybe technically I do have a right to be angry. But choosing a hateful, angry attitude toward others, no matter how "right" I think I am, has serious consequences. Not only does it prevent me from forgiving my friend, but, as Buechner says, the skeleton at the feast is *me*. I become unable to *accept* forgiveness from my friend. Carried further, anger causes us to even scoff at God's forgiveness—to purposely refuse to be forgiven. Thomas John Carlisle illustrated this kind of anger in his poem about Jonah:

*Tantrum*

The generosity of God
displeased Jonah exceedingly
and he slashed with angry prayer
at the graciousness of the Almighty.
"I told You so," he screamed.
"I knew what You would do,
You dirty Forgiver.
You bless Your enemies
and show kindness to those
who despitefully use You.
I would rather die
than live in a world
with a God like You.
And don't try to forgive me either.[3]

Psychologists often say that anger is a secondary emotion. There is something beneath it that sets it off. In the case of forgiveness, I suspect that the basic thing in our humanity that nudges us to hate and be angry is *pride*. As Buechner points out, pride has to be swallowed to permit either forgiving or being forgiven:

To forgive somebody is to say one way or another, 'You have done something unspeakable, and by all rights I should call it quits between us. Both my pride and my principles (q.v.) demand no less. However, although I make no guarantees that I will be able to forget what you've done, and though we may both carry the scars for life, I refuse to let it stand between us. I still want you for my friend.

To accept forgiveness means to admit that you've done something unspeakable that needs to be forgiven, and thus both parties must swallow the same thing: their pride.[4]

Children seem to say they're sorry easily. When my kids were younger, it seemed an almost natural part of them. I guess it's only as we grow older that we develop and nurture pride and allow that pride to foster anger which controls our responses and reactions to friends—and blocks forgiveness.

Another thing that blocks forgiveness is guilt. Real guilt for things we've done wrong is good in the sense that it challenges us to seek forgiveness from God and others. It is only when the wrong we've done is unprocessed because of our stubborn refusal to ask forgiveness, that this kind of guilt stands in the way.

But there are other patterns of guilt, and this is where we get into trouble. One is the guilt that is a sort of conditioned response to life. It's sort of the way some of us have learned to feel about ourselves—a pardon-me-for-living attitude. This causes us to feel guilty at unlikely times. Sometimes, for example, I can be just walking down the street, or cooking dinner, and wham! All of a sudden I feel guilty, and I can't find any reason to feel that way.

Another pattern of guilt is somehow hanging onto it even after asking to be forgiven. Almost as if we can't believe it's true, or maybe forgetting that it's over with.

Guilt mostly keeps us from forgiving ourselves. But, just as anger has consequences that go both ways, so does guilt. It can block our ability to forgive our friends.

There is a kind of progressive pattern to forgiveness. To forgive a friend, I must first forgive self. To ask God's forgiveness, the prerequisite is forgiving my friend. And there's a reciprocity between the last step and the first one: To really receive God's forgiveness, I must forgive self.

We might not like this—that there are "requirements" to being forgiven by God. It really made me mad the first time someone pointed it out to me. But the Lord's Prayer *does* say: ". . . as we have forgiven others." That's past tense, too.

When Dale Bruner visited our church recently, he pointed out that we can pray the Lord's Prayer by actually inserting the name of the friend we've forgiven into that slot. That helped me to further realize how important this progressive pattern is to forgiveness. It's God's way of doing things.

So, then, the first thing necessary in learning to forgive a friend comes by learning to forgive myself, and that's tied into learning to receive God's forgiveness. This requires four steps:

The first step is to process the wrongs and the sin in our lives. This happens through confession: telling God what our sins and shortcomings are. He already knows, anyway! But a necessary part of the process is for us to articulate and acknowledge just where we have been wrong. Once we've faced up to the failures and weaknesses, and left them with God, we can stop worrying about them. Sometimes that's hard to do. It's just too much to believe that once He's forgiven us, it's all taken care of. The only thing we can do about this is to decide not to hang onto guilt and self-condemnation. To choose, daily, to remember that we are forgiven—and receive what He has given.

Secondly, we have to start setting aside false expectations and standards, and realize that what we demand of ourselves may not be what God is working on in us at this time. Being forgiven doesn't mean that all parts of us are okay—we need to learn to forgive ourselves for the parts that haven't gotten any better, despite our efforts.

I saw this personally the other day, in an unexpected way. I'd been reading the letter to the Ephesians, where, in chapter five, Paul talks about the way Christians should be new and different. I automatically went into my list of expectations about how I should be different but never seem to make it— things like not being moody and irritable, or that I should quit eating so much.

Later that day, a friend and I were chatting over coffee. My friend mentioned a mutual acquaintance who has repeatedly mistreated me. "I don't see how you can even be *nice* to her," my friend said. "I wouldn't have anything to do with someone who did that to me, even once."

That let me know that the Lord has been working to change at least one of the things wrong with me, because on my own, I'd never been able to be nice to someone who had wronged me. Seeing that helped me to understand and forgive myself for the parts of me that aren't quite right yet. (I know, though, that this doesn't let me off the hook in working on the other things. I still have to try—but with the knowledge that He is in charge of changing the inner me according to *His* standards.)

The third step of self-forgiveness is to willfully shed the kind of guilt that is a conditioned response to life. When false guilt pops up unexpectedly, we can accept it and go around with stooped shoulders. Or, we can just dump it—recognize that there is no reason for it to be there—and purposely walk away from it.

The final step is just to claim forgiveness for self. By this, I mean just act as if it's true. Even though it's hard to believe, difficult to remember, things are wrong with us, and false guilt still overwhelms us at times: We can beat it all by acting as if we are self-forgiving.

Having self-forgiveness enables us to progress to learning how to forgive our friends.

I think it's a good idea, at this point in the progression, to establish a goal to work toward. My personal goal concerns my basic attitude toward friends. I would like to learn to approach others with a generalized *spirit* of forgiveness—rather than waiting for some specific event or action to require forgiving. And, when there is something specific in a friendship that calls for forgiveness, I'd like to move to a point where I am so aware of my own wrong that my friend's wrong becomes insignificant. Forgiving her is automatic.

In some friendships it's easy to put my goal into action.

When there is a basic camaraderie between myself and my friend, I find it rather simple to have a spirit of forgiveness concerning everything my friend does. And when such a friend and I clash, it's no big thing.

Just recently, a rather new friend (whom I've enjoyed immensely) and I clashed. The tension between us was a bit high. But, because I like her and feel really good about our friendship, I could say, "So, we've had our first clash. The first of many, probably." Then I could apologize for the wrong I'd done, and not care about what she'd done in this instance— although she responded anyway with her own apologies. The clash was over and settled simply and directly.

But a spirit of forgiveness is not always so easy, nor is the way out of the clash always so direct. When there have been past bad experiences with a friend, or when a friend is so hostile that he cannot accept my apology even when I give it, putting my goal into action is difficult. I have very few friendships where this goal is a reality, and I suspect that not many people have found it simple to put ready forgiveness into action.

But we can learn some techniques that will move us closer to the goal of having a spirit of forgiveness—and will help us when there is a specific act that requires forgiving.

This kind of forgiveness means loving in spite of what a friend does. Paul Tillich says that this kind of forgiving requires forgetting:

Forgiving presupposes remembering. And it creates a forgetting not in the natural way we forget yesterday's weather, but in the way of the great "in spite of" that says: I forget although I remember. Without this kind of forgetting no human relationship could endure healthily. . . . I speak of the lasting willingness to accept him who has hurt us. Such forgiveness is the highest form of forgetting, although it is not forgetfulness. The stumbling block of having violated another is pushed into the past, and there is the possibility of something new in the relationship.

Forgetting in spite of remembering is forgiveness.[5]

My friend Ruth told me that forgiveness has become possible for her just by making a basic decision to forgive. She said she'd always been critical and angry when faced with conflict. But then one day as she read the Beatitudes, Ruth saw herself as Jesus saw her. She decided to change. During conflict, she's learned to recognize the signs warning her that critical anger is coming. The signs are like little red flags popping up in her mind, Ruth says. Then she goes out, drives around in the car or walks on the beach until she understands what caused the clash with her friend. Then she just decides to forgive.

Often, Ruth says, once she's decided to forgive her friend, she discovers that she's the one who really needed to be forgiven—because there'd been some selfishness in her which helped to cause the conflict. Then she has to decide again—to swallow her pride and ask her friend's forgiveness.

Sometimes forgiveness requires that we are willing to look wrong, even when what we've done seems far less serious than what our friend has done.

This requires an honest evaluation of the wrong we have committed in a situation. Because we tend to have blind spots where our mistakes are concerned, even when we feel we've done no wrong, it's good to search out our motives and think about our part in the conflict. It's helpful, too, to ask the Lord for a conscience for the wrongs we've done. He'll let us know!

When a friend on a committee started bossing me—telling me how to do the job that was assigned me—I was boiling mad. She called me one day and just listed the ways I was to do things, and when. I wasn't exactly nice in my responses to her over the phone. In fact, I was a little snippy. And angry for days.

Her wrong *did* seem more serious than mine. She was manipulating me, pushing me around, making me feel inadequate. My snooty remarks seemed small in comparison.

But then I had to take the car for repairs, unexpectedly. I had no chance to get together the usual stack of books and paraphernalia that I take along for such waiting periods. So I was left to just thinking and praying.

Somehow in this process, the subject of my angry feelings toward the friend who'd been so bossy came up. And in a different way. Christ showed me that I had been wrong to be snippy no matter what she'd done. And that I needed to apologize for the wrong *I'd* done, even if it looked to her like I was taking the blame for all the wrong in the situation. I had to just let her off the hook, and let her wrongs against me be *her* responsibility. Then I could stop being angry, and forgive her—although I'm certain that to her, it looked like I was the one totally wrong!

At times, in order to forgive, we must set aside ill-feelings and be willing to act in spite of those feelings. The real test of whether forgiveness has taken place cannot be measured by feelings. It's pretty natural to have bad feelings and to be a little reluctant with a friend if we've had a serious clash. It takes time for the friendship to feel comfortable again. In a case like this, the way we act is the measure of whether forgiveness has truly happened.

My friend told me she continued to have negative thoughts and feelings toward her neighbor long after the conflict had been worked out and apologies made on both sides.

But then one day the neighbor's child became ill at school, and my friend found she was able to act in spite of her ill-feelings. Not knowing how to reach her neighbor who was out shopping, my friend took the child home and cared for him that afternoon. It was then she knew that forgiveness sometimes was more the way she acted than the way she felt.

But, when forgiveness has actually taken place, we often find that we are on the other side of the fence, feelingwise: Where once we hated, we feel compassion; we are softened.

Another friend told me that she had moved to the other side of the fence where her parents were concerned. "It was a process," she says. "Forgiveness was really a bitter pill for me to swallow. I wanted to hold onto my hate because they had wronged me. What benefits did forgiveness hold for me? Even after a year of counseling with my pastor, I had to willfully forgive—it took determination. Then I began to see some of the good my parents had accomplished in my life. But it was not until my brother visited me a few months ago that I realized how far I'd come. He was all tied up with hostility for our parents, and in him I saw where I used to be. I also found myself defending our parents—trying to explain to my brother why they'd done what they had, what made them the way they are, and so forth. It was a beautiful experience to know I could feel such deep compassion for the very people I once hated."

Forgiving also means *not* waiting for a friend to ask forgiveness. That might never happen. Perhaps our friend has no idea that he's hurt us, or to what extent the injuries harmed us. To sit around stubbornly waiting for him to see what he's done only prolongs the conflict and causes us to lick our wounds.

When a friend acts as if nothing has happened between us after the conflict, and doesn't appear to know we've been hurt, we just have to *forgive*. Just as Jesus forgave the man let down through the roof on his pallet. The man didn't ask, but Jesus knew what to do. He simply forgave.

My friend Debbie found, in the situation with her pastor, that she just needed to forgive. The biggest block for her was that she expected Reverend Worth to ask her forgiveness. She sat around for almost three years waiting.

"I'd done all the other things," Debbie recalls. "I had recognized my anger and my desire to hold onto my hurt feelings, and lick my wounds. I prayed about it and asked Jesus to take away my bad feelings. I felt I'd processed the sin, and I felt I was willing to be wrong. I saw my wrongness basically as holding onto the hurt. I wanted to forgive, and I willfully tried to do so. But forgiveness wouldn't happen for me.

"The day that I realized I could wait a lifetime and Reverend Worth would never ask my forgiveness—because he didn't even realize he'd hurt me—was the day the barriers came down. I saw that I had not allowed myself to like him or to support his ministry because of my expectations. I needed to stop waiting and start forgiving.

"But I had to figure a way to carry out that forgiveness," Debbie recalls. "Just to walk up to Reverend Worth, and tell him I forgave him, when he didn't feel a need to ask, seemed like dragging up skeletons—his and mine. But after all this time, I needed, for myself, to take some action, to put my forgiveness into some tangible form."

Debbie realized that the desire to receive forgiveness has to come from the other person. To lay our forgiveness on a friend who apparently has no idea he or she has hurt us, may just put us right at the front door, fighting the defenses. The back-door way, when a friend doesn't realize he's hurt us, is to find a way to put the forgiveness into some external action. That enables us to express the forgiveness without harming our friend. But it requires thinking about what action will express what we feel in a satisfactory way.

For Debbie, this meant volunteering to work on a new mission program which Reverend Worth had proposed. She chose this action because she felt it was an expression of support to his ministry and because it would allow her to work closely with him, allowing time to rebuild the friendship. She didn't expect quick results, but only two days after she'd signed up for the project, the wounds Debbie had licked for three years just disappeared.

"It was wonderful," Debbie says. "I'm sure the Lord just took those hurts away once I was willing to be serious about this forgiving business."

Finally: A spirit of forgiveness is a gift from God. It's not something we can muster up entirely on our own. Whenever the mental garbage cans get too full for us to drag out to the curb, we need to remember that God's love is stronger than any feeling or any blocks to forgiveness which we might have. Taking our inability to forgive to God in prayer is just the same as putting the physical garbage on the curb for disposal.

Through prayer, God replaces the garbage with forgiveness. But that's just one reason why prayer is a good back-door strategy in friendship.

# EIGHT

## Prayer/Solitude: Central Processing

Only recently did I learn that I'd had misconceptions about how the human nervous system functions.

I knew that the nerve cells transmitted and processed impulses concerning body needs, and a few other oversimplified facts. But I'd visualized it all incorrectly, thinking that nerve cells throughout the body connected together in little "chains" leading to the brain, which just had a bigger bunch of cells in one place for the more difficult processes.

So I was astounded to learn that the bodies of almost all nerve cells are *inside* the brain and spinal cord. With a few exceptions, it's only nerve fibers, not cells, that run throughout our bodies carrying messages to and from the cell bodies that process the information. All the processing is centrally located. It's interesting, too, that the place *where* the nerve fibers join the central system is at the *back* of our bodies. The first connections to cell bodies are made in the spinal cord.

In a similar manner, Christ is the center of our friendships. Through prayer, He processes what happens between friends and facilitates the connections that put us inside a friend's life.

Prayer, then, is a vital part of a back-door strategy, speeding and intensifying the intimacy necessary for friendship.

The centering process of friendship produces twofold results: It prepares me to be a better friend and strengthens the connections between me and my friend.

First, prayer prepares me to be a better friend. Maybe being "prepared" seems somewhat unnecessary. After all, isn't the only requirement just *wanting* to be a friend? Doesn't the desire to give my best to the friendship prepare me enough?

I don't think so. For one thing, Jesus Himself seemed to need times of preparation—when He went off by Himself to pray. If He needed prayer and times of preparation, how much more do I!

When I do not pray, I am less effective as a friend because I am wrapped up in myself. The human mind can pay attention only to one thing at a time. If my focus is on self, for whatever the reason, I will not be able to respond to my friend's needs—if I'm even aware that she *has* needs. Prayer prepares me to be a better friend by gradually replacing this self-centeredness with Christ-centeredness.

Self-centeredness can focus itself on past, present or future. Whatever the focus, processing it through prayer can change it and prepare me to be more effective in my friend's life.

Prayer changes the past by putting it into its proper perspective. Dwelling in the past, lurking around in things that are finished, usurps all my attention. Praying helps me to put the past back there where it belongs. (I don't mean to oversimplify here. Sometimes counseling is necessary.) When seen in it's proper perspective, I can glean information from past mistakes and experiences that might apply now to my life or my friend's life. By processing this information through Christ, it can become a positive, constructive force. Instead of sitting around rooted in my past, I can be free to help my friend deal with her past.

Self-centeredness can focus itself in the present when I choose to go it alone. Prayer can keep that from happening, but sometimes I get so busy that I unconsciously make the choice to live my life without centering on Christ. I put off prayer and live for myself. This is how it worked once:

I knew I was overextending myself, but I thought I could handle it. It began in November when Neal had a two-week vacation at home. I was slightly frazzled at the beginning of vacation because I'd just finished a mid-term in a mind-blowing course. Then there were extra meals to prepare, and some side-trips we wanted to make. I just added these into my already busy schedule, without dropping a thing. We'd planned to redecorate the bathroom during the vacation, too—just a "simple" little project of new wallpaper, new floor and new faucet. Well, the simple escalated into a major disaster when we discovered that the sink had rusted through. All the plumbing below it disintegrated when we tried to remove the old faucet. To complicate things further, there was no replacement sink manufactured any longer in the same size. After dozens of phone calls and trips to plumbing supply houses, we finally had to alter the cabinet to fit the new sink.

By this time I was running as fast as I could go. Little by little I began to neglect communicating with Christ. Prayer and quiet time could wait, I told myself. Surely the Lord would understand just how much I had to get done.

And so, self-centeredly, I went on. One excuse piled on another: shopping for horse supplies for Sharon's birthday, baking a horse-shaped birthday cake, Thanksgiving, finals in my two classes, shopping for Christmas, writing a poem for the cards and getting them addressed, baking and preparing for the big day.

All the time I kept complimenting myself for not falling apart. I knew I was living under a high potential for being stressed, but I did not *feel* stressed. I kept plugging—I mean running along, promising myself that I'd take some time before Christmas to pray and reflect on the meaning of Christ's birth to the world, and more specifically, to my life.

But the time never materialized. On the twenty-sixth, I felt stunned. Christmas was over and had passed me by, as if it hadn't happened. I went through the rest of the holiday activities like a zombie, feeling left out and disappointed. (Not until later did I realize that I was the one who had passed by Christmas.)

Worse yet, I could no longer compliment myself on not falling apart. My self-centered going it alone had finally taken its toll. I was a mess. One of the worst parts of it was that in January, when a dear friend whom I hadn't seen in two years visited, I was numb, and totally unprepared to be her friend. I could barely communicate with her.

Since then, I've learned that no matter how much I have to do, processing the present needs through Christ in prayer frees my attention from self—and allows me time, even in a crowded schedule, to be a friend.

When self-centeredness focuses on the future, it keeps my attention there instead of here. Future doesn't always mean twenty-five or thirty years from now, either. I never have trouble worrying about retirement years. But, as I sit here right now, I can get in a real tizzy about next Monday when I have to take my car in to have the bushings in the steering system repaired, dig up the money to pay for it, somehow find a ride to La Jolla in the morning, and get Shar to the orthodontist late in the afternoon. Processing all this through prayer keeps me centered on Christ. I can then make the plans for next Monday, and put it all on the shelf until the day arrives. And I'll be really present with the friends I see today.

The result of centering on Christ, allowing Him to process my past, present and future, someday will result—I hope!—in getting all of myself oriented toward Him. My ideal is that prayer be an undergirding force in my life, controlling all my actions, reactions and responses to my friends. I really aim to make prayer more constant and continuous.

Of course, it doesn't always work that way yet. Sitting here typing, I remembered that I'd begun my day without prayer. Today, while trying to write a chapter about how praying affects friendships! Whoops, better start my day over!

It comforts me that other people either have times when they forget to pray or when it seems difficult to "get through" to the Lord. Once when I was feeling distant, I was reading Paul Tournier and stumbled onto this paragraph—exactly what I needed to hear:

> Like the human dialogue, this dialogue is seen to be inter-
> mittent. Even the greatest saints have their times of drought, when
> God seems to be afar off. But the important thing about these mo-
> ments of communion with God is not that they happen but rarely,
> like flashes of lightning in the night, but that with all their solemn
> richness they do happen, and that they mean more for our whole
> life and person than years of automatic existence. These moments
> are decisive—in the full meaning of the term—in determining our
> future. They are the crossroads where we take a new direction.
> Our life thereafter will depend on them.[1]

The kind of prayer that prepares me for friendship has a dimension beyond "talking to the Lord," though. Prayer in the form of a simple dialogue begins the process. But to be truly prepared to be a better friend, I need to block out times in my schedule for an extended form of prayer: solitude.

As a child, solitude was a natural and special part of my life. I used to go off to the peach orchard in the summer and smush down a place in the two-foot high weeds, just big enough for me.

The peach orchard was ideal because it was behind the barn, and so I could go there unobserved, and even if my head peeked above the weeds, no one could see me. Not being seen is important in a family of eight: Someone might want to join me, or worse yet, find some work for me to do!

I stayed there, in the peach orchard, for what now seems hours. I made tons of dandelion chains. Being a bit perfectionistic even then, I had a definite way to do this. Only dandelions with very long stems would do. I picked them off as close to the ground as possible, pinched off the flower top, and then measured all the stems against each other to make certain they were the same length. I did all the pinching with fingernails, of course. I still remember how sticky my fingers got, and the ugly greenish-brown color. But with the pinching done just right, the top end fit perfectly into the ground end of the stem. Linked together, they made lovely chains with same-sized links.

But, my real purpose in going to the peach orchard was not to make dandelion chains. I went there instead for solitude. Time to sort out all my childish concerns and prepare myself for living.

As I grew older, I either forgot or repressed my need for solitude. I put it away, I suppose thinking it was part of the childish things. Busy with children and house and a million chores, and feeling rather indispensable, I couldn't permit myself time alone even though I sometimes had a yearning for solitude.

Giving oneself permission is probably the most difficult hurdle to cross in planning times of solitude. Being "indispensable" is only one reason. Another thing I had to struggle with was: "What will other people think?" Going off alone is not exactly accepted practice for homemaker/mothers in our society. The first time I checked into a motel alone I was certain that the desk clerk would think I was having an affair. For women—or men—in business who travel, maybe going off alone is not so threatening—but time away from work and family is difficult to carve out.

Another part of the decision concerning time is the frequency of solitude times. How often we need time alone is a matter of personality. Neal almost never needs time alone. I need much more than I allow myself. I think occupation and schedule affect the need for solitude, too. When I'm engaged in creative tasks, I find I need time alone for replenishing and regrouping myself.

But it's really important for people like me who need a large amount of solitude to find ways to be alone without disrupting the family situation. I've done this by planning little times of solitude into my schedule. Arthur Gordon, in *A Touch of Wonder,* calls this "purposeful pausing." My aim is to pause like this for a time or two every day. I often fall short of my aim. But I've found that not carving out the little times for solitude leads to a crisis situation where I *have* to get away.

I've found bits of solitude in several places. Sometimes I drive to the beach and have my lunch sandwich there. Fifteen or twenty minutes of quiet reflection soothes me. Another place of solitude is at my sewing machine. I used to sew for creativity alone. Now that I have other ways of expressing my creativity, I no longer sew for that reason. Over the years, sewing has become so automatic for me that I now find a new kind of creativity in it: I do some "creative brooding" while putting a dress together. And in the swimming pool, surrounded by people, the repetitiveness of doing lap after lap puts my brain in neutral; I feel totally alone. Then there are those rare moments when I can utilize waiting times—for car, doctor, whatever—for bits of solitude. That takes concentration, though, and I'm just beginning to be able to do it.

When planning an extended period of solitude, a "wilderness experience," I've found it very necessary to prepare my family. I plan ahead, so the kids know what I'm doing and when. Even as teenagers they like to know what I'm up to.

Also, I make a special effort to see that all their physical needs will be met while I'm away. Not quite as well as when I'm home—they have to cook for themselves! But I plan menus and write out recipes, and keep it simple. I just try to make everything about my being away as easy as possible for them.

I try to make things easy for me, too. I take along all the things I consider my "creature comforts": my Bible, journal, favorite foods, needlepoint, a book or two to stimulate my thinking. And I leave home noisy distractions: radio, TV, anything that might interrupt me.

The length of time I plan for extended periods of solitude varies according to my needs and schedule. I started short. The first time I went away only part of the weekend. But as I've learned to be more comfortable about carving out time from everything else, I try to go once a year for a five- or six-day time alone.

The place of solitude is important, also. At first I chose motels because I felt safest there and unsure about being *too* alone. I haven't quite progressed to going off to the real wilderness as some of my male friends do. But now I go off to a friend's mountain cabin, where I am all alone. I take Junior for barking. (I can't say protection: He hides behind my legs at the slightest suggestion of trouble. But he makes a lot of noise and sounds vicious.) Also, the sheriff lives across the street from the cabin, making me feel terribly safe.

Loneliness didn't bother me at all when I went away for only a day or two. But on my first five-day solitude, I had to put the lonelies away. The family went with me to the cabin for the weekend, and I planned to stay the following week and go home Friday. They left on Sunday afternoon, and as they drove off, I felt overcome with loneliness. A large portion of my life was driving off in that car, without me. It was almost as if I'd lost my place in the family. Was I doing the right thing? If I had focused on that lonely feeling, I would have ruined my wilderness experience for sure, and maybe wouldn't have completed it. Being basically comfortable about being alone made it easier for me to choose to put the loneliness into the perspective of the temporary. The five days were deliciously silent and productive.

By productive, I do not mean in tangible results. It's important for me to say that, because learning not to have expectations of myself during times of solitude was a growing process for me. I used to think I had to "accomplish something" with the time. That's partly because I'm married to the clock.

I discovered my problem with the clock mainly by having to cope with another world where time doesn't count. The ranch where Sharon's pony lives is a totally unscheduled place. There is no sense of time of day. Just day and night. If something needs to be done and isn't, there's no crisis. Tomorrow will do. My first few trips to the ranch put me in touch with my neurotic attachment to the clock.

One Saturday morning when Shar and I went to the ranch, the horses were not rounded up. I found myself stomping around, hopping from one leg to another, and then pacing up and down. Where were those horses? I wanted to get back to my schedule. The ironic part was that the whole family was going to be gone that day, and I had absolutely nothing I *had* to do. My only plan was to curl up with a good book when I got home, and enjoy a quiet day. Already I was unquiet because of my attitude.

This experience helped me to see that I actually was making time a god. Even being late for something seemed like a moral weakness to me. Knowing this helped me to put the clock into a more proper perspective. I'm not saying I have it there all the time. But I have been able to put the clock into its rightful place at least for my times of wilderness.

The other thing that caused me to have expectations of my solitude comes, I think, out of the old basic work ethic. I could not allow myself to be alone unless I was doing something. (Maybe that's why I made dandelion chains when I went off to the peach orchard as a child.) So, at first, when I went away, I felt obligated to have something to show for the time. If I hadn't written something, or read five or six books, I at least thought I had to have some new insight into myself or some new understanding to share with my family and friends. Something to show that I'd put the time to very good use.

Only slowly did it dawn on me that the productiveness of my wilderness experience cannot be measured in the tangible, or even in the intangible of insights and understandings. There is no way to measure what happens to me during solitude. But there is an immeasurable something that happens. Somehow, as I go off alone to reflect and meditate and pray, Christ gets into my life in all the deep places. There is a quieting and serenity that sets in on me. The only thing that comes close to describing this feeling is that it's like a tree well-watered.

I love the manzanita trees surrounding my friend's mountain cabin. Whenever I'm there I give the manzanitas a good soaking. I question whether or not they need the watering because the wild manzanitas in the area seem to survive without my help. (Maybe just as I can *survive* without solitude, but I'm better for having it.)

A lovely, shapely manzanita stands right outside the kitchen window of the cabin, and there's a bird feeder hanging from the branches. One morning, hours after I'd watered this tree, I was sitting at the kitchen table sipping coffee and watching the variety of birds as they fluttered around in the tree. They were more active than usual, some of them even dangling upside down from the branches. There were more of them than I'd seen at one time before, and their tiny chirping voices made a real chorus. I watched carefully, and was absolutely delighted by what I saw:

That manzanita tree had thirstily soaked up the water I'd

given. But the water was not kept and stored away only for itself. Each of its tiny oval leaves held one or two drops of water. Those lucky birds who were splashing and frolicking had something to chirp about: The tree, well-watered, seemed purposefully to be holding out its leaves to share its wealth.

There's a kind of wealth like that which comes to me in solitude, and like the manzanita, I can only share it. It's too great, too much, to be kept to myself. Solitude finishes what prayer begins: Centered on Christ, I am whole enough that I can let go of self-centeredness and hold out my hand to my friend.

The second result of prayer concerns the connections between friends. There is a binding that takes place between two friends, even without Christ. It's not impossible to have friends without Him. But, putting Him at the center of our friendships and processing all that happens between us facilitates and strengthens those bonds. Whether this is done by praying separately for a friend or praying together, making connections through Christ's love intensifies the experience of friendship and produces bonds which are both secure and enduring.

I have a whole list of friends for whom I pray. I was surprised by the length of my list when I started just jotting down names the other day. I find it helpful to write the names down occasionally just to jog my memory, but I hadn't done it for a while. In making my list this time, I was purposely brooding over what difference it makes that I pray for those people—some of them very casual friendships, some closer, some of them praying for me, too, and some of them nonpraying people.

Best of all about praying for friends is that it makes me really grateful for each one of them. Just thanking the Lord first of all for the particular friend I'm praying for deepens my appreciation of that person. Friends are a special and wonderful gift from the Lord. But it's all too easy to take the giftedness of friendship for granted.

I suppose I could say I've always been thankful to a certain extent for my friends, and I can remember giving thanks for them at times. But I really started being serious about this only recently when one of my friends started telling me that she thanks the Lord for me. That impressed me so much that I began daily saying thanks for each friend as I begin my prayer for that person. The outgrowth of doing this is a deepened affection for my friends. And although I am still often reluctant or negligent in expressing my gratitude, it's slowly becoming easier to say, "I give thanks for you."

Also, praying for my friends gives me a feeling of hopefulness, both for the friendship and for my friend. For the friendship because there are times of stress, conflict, hostility or even apathy between any two people. On my own, I might tip over like a sailboat with too much wind. Centering the friendship through prayer, even in the most difficult situation, works. The reason it works, in "sailboat language," is because it allows time to get the sails down, wait for the boat to come to an upright position, then raise the sails again, properly reefed (tied down, so the sail area is smaller) for heavy winds. Instead of being overpowered by a problem in the friendship, that problem becomes the wind that gives me sail —and the certainty of hope when all looks dreary.

Centering through Christ also offers hope for a friend when that person is struggling.

For example, a long-time friend who lives in another city called me the other evening. She had sad news. Her teenaged daughter had run away from home. With three teenagers, I could quickly understand how my friend felt. It would have been so easy to get caught focusing on the burden and be negative in my response. I almost did but caught myself. To have done that would have only added to my friend's feelings of being overwhelmed. Instead, processing the problem quickly through Christ as I listened to her helped me to just love and encourage my friend.

One thing I've discovered in praying for my friends is that there must be an element of release in my requests.

This is necessary, first of all, because none of us can do everything for a friend. Certain things are between an individual and God. We don't have the power to change our friend in those areas, or even to know what it is that's best for her. Just think of what God spared the world by not giving us that power: We'd sure mess things up if we could control each other!

Another reason for praying and releasing a friend is that I might not be the person the Lord has chosen to minister in that person's life. To feel that I must minister to all my friends at all times is arrogant. Even if I had the ability, I haven't the time. God may have someone special set aside who will speak or act in just the right way at the exactly right time. Releasing my friend to the Lord allows that to happen.

Not releasing a friend as we pray might mean that we prevent God's work in her life from happening. This can be difficult especially if we care deeply for our friend. We begin to beg the Lord for what we think this friend needs. This kind of begging, I think, can block the Lord's work in giving that friend what she really *does* need (even if it does happen to be the same need that *we* see).

This was illustrated a few months ago when a Bible teacher asked people in his audience to stand up and make a commitment of their lives to Christ. A man I know told me the following story:

"For years I've prayed that a particular friend would make a commitment to the Lord. I finally had talked this friend into coming to Bible class with me, and when the teacher asked

people to stand, I prayed like crazy, begging Christ to touch his heart. He needed the Lord so much.

"Suddenly, I was aware that the woman next to me stood. She was the wife of another friend, whom I knew had been praying for her in much the same way I'd been praying for my non-believing friend. I stopped my begging, and praised God, rejoicing for my friend's wife. At that very moment, my needy friend stood, and accepted Christ. I felt tears running down my cheeks as I welcomed him into the Body of Christ. But those tears were not just for joy. There was also, for me, the revelation that I'd almost prevented my friend's response today, and that maybe I had stood in the way of his commitment all along. It taught me to stop begging the Lord for what I see anyone needs. I just pray and leave it up to Him."

Praying for a friend strengthens the bonds even while we are absent from one another, no matter how great the distance. I have friends way across the country whom I have not seen for years. But prayer has kept those friendships fresh and alive. If we'd see each other today, it would be as if those years hadn't separated us physically.

During illness, prayer while absent is extremely bonding. As I type this, my father is critically ill, and I am in Ohio to be with him, separated from my friends by something like 2,500 miles. But the prayers of my California friends have followed me and comforted me. The distance hasn't mattered.

"Prayer from a distance" has actually developed into a ministry for my friend Ann, who is separated not by miles, but illness. Ann has rheumatoid arthritis, a progressive disease that strikes the joints and then goes on to attack every system of the body. Several years ago, the disease attacked Ann's nervous system, and she nearly died. It was then that she first found that Christ was real in her life. She learned to pray when her pastor suggested that if she could find even one

square inch of her body which was free from pain, to thank God for that.

Out of that experience Ann has learned to pray all the time, for everything. Because of her illness, she's been able to make friends with people who might not let a physically capable person into their lives. People who are ill or handicapped accept her friendship, sometimes even seek it out, simply because they know Ann understands their predicament. Daytimes, she is on her bedside phone, listening to her friends. Then she stays awake long into the night, praying for them.

All this about praying for friends may seem fairly simple. But the hardest part, for some of us, is *remembering*. It's taken me a long time to find ways to better jog my memory on this. One way is the list that I mentioned earlier. Another is that I do not promise someone that I will pray unless I really mean it. Glib, easily made promises just glide right out of my brain as fast as they do from my mouth. When I sincerely say I'll pray for a friend, I'm more likely to follow through.

It's been really helpful to me to use little association games to bring to my memory the friends I'm praying for. The latest, and I think the best, of these that I've come up with so far is car color. Every time I see a yellow car, I pray for Patty. Brown is Christy, light blue for Peg, and so on. (Not only does it mean more prayers for my friends—it improves my driving. I find it terribly difficult to screech at other drivers while I'm talking to the Lord.)

But even more special and more binding than praying *for* a friend is the experience of praying *with* him.

Praying aloud with my friends—just two of us or maybe three—has not come easily for me. First, I find it a little scary. There just doesn't seem to be any way to avoid intimacy while praying with someone. Add to that my inability to be quickly articulate: listening to the prayers of those who are more verbally oriented than I (that's almost everyone I know!), I often

feel a little unnecessary. It seems my verbal friend has said it all so much better and smoother than I could have.

How does a person like me, who thinks and speaks slowly, learn how to pray with a friend? Three things have helped:

One is my basic decision to step beyond any fears I have concerning intimacy. I *do* want to allow my friends inside my life to know me—and I do want to be in their lives, making a difference because I'm there. When that seems fearful, the only thing that works is to recognize the fear and set it aside and pray anyway.

Another thing concerns my attitude about what prayer is. I've had to overcome my discomfort about my inarticulateness by remembering to whom I'm praying. Not to my friend, but to the Lord. I suspect that He doesn't differentiate between lovely, flowing verbal masterpieces and my halting, stumbling, poorly chosen words. And, in my experience, the friends who pray with me don't seem to mind my slowness, either.

But the most important part of praying aloud with a friend has been *practice*. Just doing it makes it easier. Praying together profoundly affects the depth of a friendship. There seems to be a kind of deepening cycle that is set off when friends pray together. The resulting intimacy leads to deeper sharing, which, in turn, leads to more frequent prayer—continually drawing us closer together.

This closeness is nice to live with. It means I can ask my friend for almost anything or share things that no one else cares about. Because she already knows much about me, I need to say very little to her about my concerns. She responds quickly and accurately.

Probably the most practical thing that happens when two of us pray together is that we develop the ability to *be* the other person's faith. By that, I mean believing for him when he cannot believe for himself.

Being the faith for a friend really makes a difference in a

tight situation. Sometimes a problem is so consuming that believing there is an end to it or a way out is just impossible. But a friend, standing by, able to visualize the problem solved and the person made more whole, can do the believing through these times.

My friend Patty and I have experienced this several times throughout our years of praying together. We're tied together by other things than prayer—same age, children of similar ages, mutual friends, common interests—but all those bonds have been strengthened by our central connection through Christ. Her faith for me has not only been practical, but has been instrumental in keeping me going—especially during the early years of my Christian life. And when she's felt distant from the Lord, or has a consuming problem, it's turned around. I become her faith for a time. There's a joy in doing that for each other.

It's difficult—probably impossible—to say just how much prayer affects a friendship. Words like depth, closeness, intensity, only begin to express the binding quality that centering in Christ brings to the experience of being friends.

None of us can know, except by experiencing it, what praying together does for us as friends. The results will be unique to the persons involved: because we've processed everything that happens between us through Christ—the Creator-center of friendship.

# NINE

## Touch:
## A Bridge Between Friends

A couple years ago two friends and I decided upon an adventure. We wanted to do something "different."

So, for that year, we agreed to take turns choosing a restaurant once a month for lunch. The qualification for selection of a given place was that it must be slightly "far-out."

My friend June was the all-time winner for selecting a tiny restaurant at the beach—so small that she wasn't certain that we'd found the right one.

We were the only customers. We sat on stools at a counter and were given a cup of herb tea. It tasted so bad that I wondered if I were being poisoned or drugged. Our guru host asked us not to talk while he prepared our lunch because it might disturb his creative efforts. Jackie, who loves to talk, kept asking him questions and chatting anyway. His response to her was to ask if we wanted a small, medium or large lunch. No, there was no menu. He assured us that we'd like what he was making. By this time I was plenty apprehensive, especially after the tea. Maybe this adventure thing was more than I wanted. I soon found out that it *was* more than I *needed*.

The guru decided that what we needed was to relax before lunch. He brought out a young man whom he introduced as his student. We were to be the recipients of a *free* shoulder massage—whether or not we wanted one. All we had to do was close our eyes (and our mouths) and relax.

Relax was the last thing I felt like doing. I wanted to get out of there. I'd never seen this young man before. How dare he *touch* me? Thrown off guard because he did not first *ask* my permission, it did not even occur to me that I could have refused.

I survived the shoulder massage with only a few more knots in my shoulder muscles than when he began—and some insights about how much touch threatened me.

The lunch that followed the massage was quite delicious: a combination of fruits and nuts. A table was carried outside so we could enjoy the beauty of the ocean. The spoons and food were passed out the window, and the guru and all his students joined us to "rap." Jackie tried to convert the guru, but he told her he was already a Christian. June invited one of the students to Bible study. I just sat there with my mouth open, dumbfounded by the adventure of it all.

I don't think I am unique in being threatened because a young man in a restaurant touched me without asking my permission. Touch can be a very threatening thing to many of us. This, I think, is because we fail to understand that the skin really has two functions. It serves as a kind of boundary, to keep us all in one place. That, we can accept and appreciate: It saves us from blooping around like amoebas. But the other function, touching and being touched, which *bridges* us to other people, is either ignored or misunderstood.

Some of us even get a little neurotic about the boundary. We extend it out way beyond our skin, like an imaginary property line way out past the front door of our lives. And just as someone trying to get in the front door is fended off, so a person crossing the property line is in trouble. That's our territory.

Territoriality is a natural instinct in animals. This instinct is so strong that sometimes even the normal relationship between species is reversed. Our Siamese cat, Charisma, chases away dogs many times larger than she is if they even *look* as if they might consider stepping on our driveway. That's her domain.

But a need for territory in humans is not natural and instinctual. We have no inborn need for space. We have acquired "learned" property lines, which show up in many ways.

We each express our territoriality in some distinct manner. A man's chair may be his inviolate possession. That's a kind of "standing societal joke." But women also have their spots. I "own" one end of the living room sofa, and I always feel a little put out when I walk into the room and see one of the kids flaked out in my spot—especially if that's where I was headed! I also feel strongly possessive about my kitchen if someone comes in uninvited and tries to boss me around or gets too much under my feet. I am the "resident expert" there, and so infringement on my territory has the additional potential of damaging my pride.

People who are less territorial often stand too close when they talk. They really violate the property lines of the rest of us. A guy I used to work with was disliked by almost everyone in the lab. He was a nice, thoughtful guy, but when he spoke to another person, he always stood very close and leaned right into the other person's face. I used to watch the reactions: everything from facial expressions of discomfort, to leaning backward or stepping away. (And he didn't even have bad breath!)

Reactions to property line infringement vary with person-

ality. I usually slink away, try to withdraw, as I did in the
beach restaurant. But some people go so far as to react hos-
tilely or aggressively.

For example, when I took a one-day workshop class, one of
the men there, whom I will call Jacob, shared an interesting
experience. He was standing next to his boss while the two of
them conducted a seminar. The boss raised his arm to point at
a chart so that his arm was right in front of Jacob's face, entirely obstructing his view of the audience. Although there
was no reason to continue pointing, the boss went on with the
lecture, continuing to hold his arm there. Rather than interrupt the lecture, Jacob gently lowered the boss's arm. The reaction was shocking, and painful: The boss turned around and
socked Jacob. Apparently his property line was easily violated
and aggressively defended.

There are only a few places in our society where property
lines are easily crossed and touch is permitted without specific
permission. One is in sexual intimacy. That's unthreatening to
most people (I think). The other place where touch is permitted is in the more hostile context of fighting or in contact
sports.

One universally acceptable form of touch is the handshake.
But even it is a kind of put-off. Probably shaking hands origi-
nated as a physical gesture to say, "I don't have a weapon."
But, actually, the hand becomes a weapon when we shake
hands because it keeps physical touch an arm's length away.

Probably at the bottom of our discomfort concerning touch
is embarrassment. Just notice all the apologies when two people bump into each other by accident. And how often have we
heard that old admonishment about not displaying affection
or emotion in public? Added to this is the fear that if we
freely touch another person of the same sex, we might be suspected of homosexuality.

This embarrassment about touch starts young, too. I can

remember going to my grandmother's house when I was little. I was her first grandchild, so had a special place in her affection. As soon as I walked through the doorway, she'd grab me up and hug me and kiss me, and say over and over, "How is Grandma's girl today?," all the while hugging and kissing me more. I used to be *so* embarrassed by all this attention and affection that I was mortified. I got to the point that I sometimes dreaded going to her house. All this before the tender age of ten—she moved to another state then, and I saw her only once or twice before her death. Her cards and letters with, "How is Grandma's girl?" and a row of X's and O's, always reminded me of my childhood embarrassment. *Now* I'm embarrassed that I felt that way! Perhaps Grandma understands those things now.

It's not surprising, though, that I was embarrassed by so much touch. The training away from touch and touching begins early in our society. Babies are born tactile creatures. As more research has been done on the importance of touch, we're progressing—going back to giving our infants plenty of physical stroking. But only a few years ago, when my children were babies, it was different. There was almost an urgency to move those little tactile creatures away from touch. Many times I was told that I was "going to spoil that baby if I did not stop holding him or her so much." When I was around such people, I sometimes went to another room to hold one of the babies to avoid being criticized.

It's difficult to define all that this has done to us as persons. It's easier to see the results in animals, because they grow up quickly. Right before our eyes, quite soon, is the outcome of their "cultural" upbringing.

Our two dogs are perfect examples of this. Junior, the oldest, came to us an already-named adult (that's why the oldest dog is called Junior!). His first year (before he came to us) was spent in a kennel with little touch and only occasional affection. As a result, he is shy, wary, and sometimes grumpy. Even after five years spent with us, and lots of patting, Junior will still only permit certain people to touch him. Nelson was a puppy when we brought him home. With his little Schnauzer haircut on that tiny body, he was irresistible. He got almost non-stop touching. The result is that Nels is exuberant and friendly almost to the point of being obnoxious. He doesn't care who touches him or when or where. Any time or place will do, and a foot is just as good as a hand. If no one offers a pat, Nels takes it upon himself to get touched: He simply leans on the nearest foot available.

Extrapolating from the effects of touch and non-touch on the personality of a dog, we can begin to see and understand just how much our early socialization away from the tactile has limited us as humans. It's almost as if we've eliminated one whole way of communication: the tactile. We walk around wearing imaginary plastic bubbles that allow only partial communication by means of the "more acceptable" senses.

Certainly, we place touch lower on the scale of importance than the four other senses just by refusing to develop the tactile. None of the senses are fully developed, of course—we're capable of much more than we experience in any area. But sight and hearing have been rated more highly significant, with probably vision being most important. We've given plenty of attention to their development. Taste and smell and touch are treated as if they're just there, but we don't really need them. Though life would be pretty boring without taste or smell, we don't *need* either of them to communicate with another person.

But we do need touch if we are to communicate fully, especially with those close to us. Touch is a necessary and special part of being friends.

But what about those of us for whom touch is threatening? (In our society, according to some statistics I read somewhere, that may be almost everyone.) Because we are limited in our ability to reach out and touch a friend or reluctant to be touched, will we be unable to form deep and lasting friendships? Will we, like my dog Junior, never get over our early socialization?

Many books I've read say that the damage is permanent. Perhaps I'm an optimist, but I don't believe that permanent-damage stuff for one minute. The reason I don't believe it to be true is because I think God created the human mind to be different than an animal's. Just because a dog or monkey or cat never progresses much beyond their early training doesn't mean people can't. Sure, God created the human mind in a way that it can be damaged or distorted by early experiences. But he also built into that same mind the ability to be redeemed. And where touch is concerned, I think that redeeming takes place by learning. Just as we once learned *not* to touch, we are capable of learning, now, *to* touch.

Because I think the first step in learning anything is understanding, I tried to find out just why our culture has opted to socialize us not to touch.

A friend who has studied in this area told me that to a large degree it's tied into the work ethic situation. The choice to lean toward and give attention to the visual and auditory forms of communication was probably an outgrowth from our desire to produce. Our society places great value on the tangible. Things we see and hear fit in okay with that, and so we naturally have developed those forms of communication. But touch is in conflict with the tangible world because it gets into the world of the emotional and arouses good feelings. That's a no-no for our society because it reduces competition to produce more than the other guy: People who feel comfortable and cared for will lose their neurotic needs to compete or be workaholics. That, in turn, reduces the total product output. It's better to keep people a little frustrated—and working harder. We haven't wanted touch because it gets in the way of what we value most: things.

I'm not certain whether my friend's explanation—or perhaps I should say my understanding of what he said—covers all the reasons for our society's making subordinate communication by touch. But it did make sense to me.

This explanation seems reasonable to me also when comparing our culture to others. There are some cultures where touch has not only been preserved as a communication form, but has been developed to the point that the society is *based* on the tactile. A former missionary to Liberia told me that the natives were totally tactile—until the missionaries or others influenced them with our values! It's difficult for us to even imagine what "totally tactile" means.

A road is not measured in miles or meters. The road is long if it is bumpy, rocky, has steep hills and is difficult to negotiate. The road is short, no matter the length, if it is an easy, non-strenuous walk. The only clocks are biological, when a need arises—or when the birds sing and wake people. There is no such thing as measuring time in discreet intervals. Three o'clock in the afternoon is just as good a time for these natives to do their work as eight in the morning is for us. And they may play all night.

Cultural differences are obvious even in our own society among those who come from other countries. My neighbor, Carmella, came here from Italy when she was nineteen. A couple years ago, she and her husband retired and moved in next door. I didn't know them very well, and I didn't know their grown children at all. But when Mike died I took dinner over after calling hours, and I was passed around the room and hugged and kissed—and then verbally thanked. The touch came before the verbal, and I loved it. A very tender moment.

But our culture is not the only thing to blame for our reluctance to touch. Some of us Christians have adopted the cultural viewpoint, and then interpreted scripture through it. We've assigned a negative connotation to the word flesh, which is used in the Bible, and placed the tactile on a level lower than non-importance. We've moved it down a notch from that to a place where it has become threatening: Anything that has to do with the physical is wrong and non-Christian, or at least, suspicious. Not only has this interpretation affirmed and intensified our cultural inclination to subordinate all tactile communication, but carried to the extreme—in some denominations—some of us have learned to view our bodies as ugly or something to be ashamed of.

I don't think that's what God intended. He created our bodies and our tactile needs. It seems to me that the Bible is in direct conflict with our negative and suspicious viewpoint concerning touch and physical things. The people of the Bible were free with their bodies and free to touch. They had no property lines out front.

This makes it necessary, if we are to learn to reach out and touch our friends, to take a look at scripture and see what it really says about touch.

First of all, I think that we have to try to discover what the Apostle Paul meant when he wrote so often about the flesh— because I think our negative connotations have been drawn from a misunderstanding of what Paul meant to say. He did use the expression "the flesh" a lot—91 times, according to my Strong's Concordance. Except for the two occasions when he used the word for the meat of animals, the Greek word Paul used for flesh was *sarx*. Part of our misinterpretation is that we have extended the meaning of *sarx* to mean the entire body and all things physical. That's incorrect, because *sarx* means only the skin or the part of the body that is external. *Soma* is the Greek word for the entire body. Paul's use of the term "flesh," my pastor-friend, Peg, tells me, was to describe the body without reference to God. That means, to me, a kind of preoccupation with the body, which leads to physical and spiritual destructiveness. Like Ephesians 2:3, *living* in the passions of the flesh—serving *sarx*, carrying out its desires and thought patterns. That's a lot different than being able to view our bodies as God's good creation and being physically free enough to reach out a hand and give a friend a pat or a hug. And, taking a second look at Paul, it's apparent that he placed high value on the body—for example, the verse in Romans 12 where he suggests we offer our bodies as an act of *worship*.

But I'd like to think Paul's choice of the word *sarx* had some underlying motives and connotations. I've thought a lot about him and pictured him, pacing the floor, thinking and writing.

When I started searching to find out more about the Biblical concept of the physical, I discovered that the Old Testament understanding of man was always man seen in relation to God. Because of this, the Hebrew concept of man was one of wholeness. Man could not be split into parts.[1] Even the Hebrew word for flesh, *bâsâr*, doesn't seem to separate body from spirit: *bâsâr*, by extension, says my Hebrew dictionary, means *person*. (I have to trust the dictionary to be right on that one, because Hebrew looks only like scratching to me!)

But the Greeks saw man only in terms of human nature, and they divided him into parts—mind, body, spirit. Out of this came the idea that one could do anything with his body, or engage in any kind of destructive behavior. So, maybe Paul used *sarx* simply to speak against that kind of living. But I'd like to think he was doing something else.

Maybe Paul was using *sarx* as a kind of picture word. He could have just preached against the list of sins, such as those listed in Galations 5:19–21, without naming them flesh. Perhaps, like a poet, Paul was looking for a word that in itself would add emphasis and help his readers to visualize more clearly what he was saying. I see him drawing together the contrasting Hebrew and Greek concepts of man, and using the flesh as a part of the whole (metonymy) to make his point. By doing this, I think Paul was saying, "between the lines": "Hey, you guys, this Greek concept of dividedness *is* right, *when* man is out of relation to God. Separated from God, the One who makes him whole, man *is* divided. He gets fragmented into parts. And just look at what trouble those separated parts can get into!"

Well, maybe my imagination of what Paul was trying to say between the lines is off base. But, it is clear to me that he did not in any way intend to say that the physical or the tactile are wrong or suspicious. And the rest of the New Testament seems to back that up.

Touch seemed to be a way of communication and an important part of healing to Jesus. I get the feeling as I read the Gospel stories about Jesus' ministry that touch may have been the most important of the five senses to Him. In just over fifteen pages of the Gospel of Mark in my RSV, I found the words touch and hand twenty-three times. Jesus touched—and people touched Him. Even when the stories about Jesus don't mention touch, it is often implied by the way that people gathered close around Him, and by the fact that they brought their sick to Him. Getting near Him seemed to be *the* thing to do.

As I read on into Acts, I saw that the disciples carried on Jesus' ministry of touching. Touch seemed to be a vital part of the life of the early church, right from the beginning. Acts 3:6–7 shows Peter healing the cripple: ". . . in the name of Jesus Christ of Nazareth, walk. And he took him by the right hand . . ." The prayer in Acts 4:30 is: ". . . while thou stretchest out thy hand to heal . . ." People brought their sick so that even the *shadow* of Peter would touch them.

Touch was not just important for healing way back then. The people involved in healing ministries today tell me that touch seems to provide a kind of bridge for the Holy Spirit's work in healing.

In a class I attended, a doctor told us that there might be physiological reasons, too, why touch aids in the healing process. He believes that touch interrupts pain. It's difficult to study pain, he said, and there are different theories of why this interruption occurs. One reason might just be that the nerve fibers carrying touch conduct faster than the ones carrying pain—thereby blocking pain. But he said that attentional factors may also be an influence in lessening the experience of pain. Since a large part of the sensory and motor area of the brain is devoted to the hand, it makes sense that touch, especially holding a person's hand, might take his or her attention away from the pain. Sometimes pain recycles even after the source of it is gone, and this doctor believes that recycling results in learned patterns of pain. It's nice to know that a learned pain pattern might be interrupted by something all of us can learn to do: touch.

And I do think all of us should be challenged to learn to touch in healing ways. I've always tended to think of healing being in a special category only for the ones who are gifted by the Spirit in that way. That is a special, gifted ministry, and I don't want to lessen it. I'm just saying that perhaps, as friends, we could learn to be a healing influence in one another's lives —sort of "preventive medicine." If my doctor friend who taught the class on pain and healing is right about learned pain patterns, we might be able to keep those patterns from being learned just by holding a friend's hand. And, in many kinds of sickness, maybe touch could help keep little things from building *into* big illnesses. Perhaps "a touch a day keeps the doctor away?" It's worth trying, anyway.

Another way touch was used in the early church was in the laying on of hands. Sometimes that was commissioning people for a special task. But, often, the laying on of hands marked the coming of the Holy Spirit into a person's life.

Some people today still receive the Holy Spirit into their lives by the laying on of hands. That's not the only way He enters a human life, of course. But the fact that the Holy Spirit sometimes comes by touch is a hint to me of what He does once He gets into our lives. Once we invite Christ, through the Holy Spirit, to reside in us, He helps us to find freedom to touch one another. He gets into all the truncated and closed off places in us, and teaches us that the tactile is part of God's good life.

For me, overcoming the reluctance to touch and be touched has been a process. The advertisement for a health spa says: "I want your body." Just so, the Holy Spirit seemed to say to me: "I want your body so that you can be free of the rigidity that keeps you from expressing yourself and reaching out to others. Together we will overcome your embarrassment of the physical and your inability to enjoy tactile communication."

After years of rigidity and embarrassment, physical freedom doesn't come easily. The first part for me was examining my misconceptions about my body.

I'd grown up feeling klutsy and stiff. I don't think I ever felt ashamed of my body, but there was a kind of subtle thing that my body wasn't too good. Some of that was a result of the not-subtle influence of some of the churches I attended as a child, with their focus on being plain, wearing no makeup, and keeping one's body well covered—long sleeved dresses even when it's 100° outside. The body was tolerated only to house the soul.

It was only slightly more difficult to grasp onto some of the other things that caused me to feel slightly ugly and uncomfortable. Our society measures people by awfully high standards. For women, those standards are met only by Playboy bunnies, and the places where my body didn't fit into the proper mold embarrassed me.

I had to look at those standards and see that the acceptance of societal standards for body causes us to fall into either body worship—placing too much emphasis on the physical, either by what is considered beautiful, or by an unhealthy preoccupation with health—or into mistreatment by overeating and such.

Changing my ideas about my body was partially motivated by a surprise. Just about the time I was beginning to examine my misunderstandings about the physical and see that I had not been born rigid, but had learned it—my mother came to visit, bringing two albums of my childhood pictures. There, before my eyes, was proof that I had been a beautiful child. I'd never known that, and had grown up thinking I wasn't attractive. Seeing how wrong I was about the child sent me to the mirror for a long, hard look at the adult. Finally, I realized that a few blemishes didn't ruin the whole creation. I started to see my body more God's way, and began to think of ways I could enjoy the physical.

This meant I had to purposely set out to find ways to loosen up. It was an experimental process, trying many things and selecting the ones that are good and comfortable to me. Of my experiments, the most fun, and maybe the most freeing, was taking belly dancing lessons. I didn't stick with it, but loved the "wild" exhilaration of belly dancing.

The way that I've discovered what physical activities are "my things" is when they interest me over a period of time. Tennis has passed the test: Even when I've dropped it temporarily because of some other interest, I've gone back to it. And, I don't see myself *ever* giving up swimming—partly because it was so hard for me to learn that I couldn't think of stopping! But, mostly, because swimming's taught me about my body and what it can do, continues to teach me and keeps me moving away from my learned rigidity.

Another thing besides learning causes physical rigidity, though. Bill Mueller, a Christian who is a masseur, explained this to me. He said our bodies become rigid when we cannot express ourselves in relationships. Bill said the muscles tighten and lock energy in, reflecting psychological struggles. Not only do our muscles stiffen like this, Bill says, but the rigidity is selective to the problem. A tightened trapezius—a muscle in the back—shows that a person is carrying a heavy load, feeling too much responsibility. When someone is defensive, the levator scapula, which lifts the shoulder blade, tenses much like a turtle pulling in his head. A shoulder muscle called the deltoid tightens when a person lacks psychological room, and so forth. Bill helps people discover the emotions causing these stiffened muscles, and gives them exercises to relieve some of the tension, helping them to move away from rigidity.

Moving away from physical rigidity, whatever its causes, is the biggest step toward learning to touch. All that's left then is practice: just reaching out a hand to touch a friend.

Practice isn't always easy. It took years before I found the courage to be the initiator in hugging my friends. I was available for hugging a long time before that, if someone else made the first step. But my ingrained embarrassment of touching and being touched was so deep that it is only recently that I've begun to feel really spontaneous about reaching out to a friend—without any "should I's?" running around in my head!

All the long, hard process of learning to touch is worth the effort. Nothing tells a friend of our care more than a touch or a hug. In fact, touch may be the only way to get inside the back door to communicate our care. When we are willing to reach out, we'll be able to call forth a response from our friend—and help her to move beyond whatever it is that holds her back.

A lady I met at a conference was a good example of how touch can communicate care. Helen told me that once she never felt cared about by anybody. She couldn't remember ever being touched by her parents. That left her with an emotional hunger so great that nothing anyone said could convince Helen she was loved. She went on for years—living scar tissue. Then an old family friend began to perceive just what was going on with her. He sat and held her as if she were a child. He became a father-substitute for Helen, giving her, through touch, the love she'd never felt before. Her face glowing, Helen told me that it worked. And, by the warm and caring way Helen reached out to the others at the conference, I'd say it worked very well!

Touch is more than just a bridge connecting skin to skin. Touch goes beyond, to get inside, serving as a bridge to communicate the inner messages for which words are inadequate. Tactile communication is the silent voice of the soul: a physical gesture that articulates the intangibles within.

Touch puts soul in contact with soul, soothing our inner isolation, connecting us in deeper ways—and teaches us that friendship is more than just skin deep.

# TEN

## Little Things: The Language of Friendship

When I signed up for a course in statistics, I expected it to be all math. Math and I have clashed ever since third grade when I had to stand at the blackboard and learn to add columns of numbers—and got a violent headache. After that, I avoided math whenever possible. So, it was with great apprehension, and only because I needed the class as a prerequisite for one I *really* wanted to take, that I registered for statistics.

I soon discovered that math, even for a math-hater, was not going to be the biggest problem in learning statistical methods —although there is some arithmetic involved. The real task was going to be learning the *language* of statistics. All kinds of symbols, unpronounceable words, charts and graphs looked worse than Greek to me when I began. (Now that I'm studying New Testament Greek, statistical language looks simple!) It took a period of time to learn the "words" and master the language of statistics, but it was fun. The fun of learning the language made even the math tolerable.

A peculiar form of language is involved in many fields of study, professions or areas of life where we might not expect it. Whether it means funny little symbols and Chi-square tests in statistics, formulas in chemistry, theological terms in the church, or whatever—it's necessary to learn the meaning of the words and then use them to communicate in that area.

Just so, there's a special kind of language in friendship that communicates concern and expresses care. The little things we do for a friend are the "words" of friendship language.

At first glance, little things may seem just that: small, unimportant, not really necessary for making and keeping friends.

But left undone, the little things are big things. In any relationship, including friendship, it's often the undone little things—petty annoyances—that build up and cause conflict and disturbances between two people.

Little things *done* build up another way. Just as words added to words make phrases, sentences, paragraphs, pages, chapters, books—little things added one to another help to build a friendship. They are the stuff friendship is built of— and a TLC way through the back door and into a friend's life.

Little things are sometimes simple, but most often these words of concern express our care more effectively than the spoken word. Something as simple as a cake baked for no special occasion has a special message for my kids: I care for you.

Although the small things we do for a friend might sometimes *seem* simple, usually there is effort involved. It might just be easier to let the opportunity to express care pass by instead of thinking about just what kind of "word" would let a friend know of our concern. This means making a firm commitment to *use* the language of little things. What appears to be the smallest of back-door strategies often requires quite a bit of imagination and creativity on our part.

Sometimes discovering the right word takes a little detective work, in the form of observation and perception. For example, a friend would have to know me pretty well to know that I am nutty about lilacs. It's not something I talk about often, especially since moving to California where lilacs are

few and far between. But the love of lilacs is deeply imbed-
ded in me, because when the lilacs bloomed back in Ohio, it
meant spring had arrived to stay—and I'd usually been waiting since October for spring! Lilacs, with their wonderful
color and extravagant fragrance, seemed the perfect tribute to
spring. My friends Anita and Jan have somehow detected my
love for lilacs, and every now and then one of them will pop
in with a bouquet. Sometimes it's a special occasion, and
sometimes not. Either way, those lilacs speak to me of my
friends' care probably more than anything else they've done.

There may be as many words in the language of little things
as there are people. Finding the best one for everyone might
not be possible. But just because we have not been able to
discover what word speaks especially to a friend, doesn't
mean we have no way to express care.

There are little things that are universally significant, touching the life of everybody. For example, a note written, even in
haste, adds a special touch to the receiver's day. Putting our
care on paper says that we are concerned enough for that
friend to do a little more than what's necessary. I have one
friend, Peg, who always adds a scripture verse or two on the
bottom of her little care-notes. I love getting a note from her,
and can barely wait to see what verses she's sent—because
somehow she chooses just what I needed to hear that day.

The telephone also has potential for being a universal word
in the language of little things. Of course, it has potential for a
lot of other things—like people trying to sell me things I don't
want, never have wanted and never will want. And, like teenaged daughters who seem to never stop talking. But I'm convinced that carving out time to just say hello by phone is a
special way to express care for my friends, although I am most
often guilty of not making the right uses of my telephone. For
example: a friend's name comes to mind. I wonder how he is
doing, or how her meeting went last night. A perfect time to

communicate my concern. And what do I do? I promise my-self that I'll phone later, after breakfast. After breakfast be-comes after lunch, and then, after dinner. A week later when I see the person I was concerned about, I remember that I meant to call. Which means nothing to my friend.

Hospitality is one of the most comfortable of the universal "little things" words. Having friends over for lunch or dinner —or just to relax and have coffee—is a good way to say we care. I have one friend, Shirley, who extends an open invita-tion for dinner one evening a week. She then prepares for a gang—and usually has one.

Eating together was often mentioned in scripture. Meals were not just times of physical nourishment, but times to be together and to enjoy one another's company.

Just so, enjoying meals together has value for friends today. It keeps our friendships fresh and up to date, and says to our friends that we care enough for them to carve time out of our day just to be together. That's special.

All little things are made more special by the addition of some creativity. Creativity, added to the desire to express care or concern, extends the meaning of our "words."

It's fairly easy, for example, to prepare dinner for another family when there is illness or something. I just usually throw it together along with whatever I'm cooking that day for my own family. With three teenagers, I cook such large quantities that I scarcely notice any difference. Even done simply like this, dinner taken to a friend expresses care. But a few crea-tive touches give it deeper meaning. For example:

A couple years ago, I was scurrying around getting the gro-cery shopping done before I had to go somewhere else. We'd just returned from vacation, so my day was more hectic than usual with all the "re-entry" chores. I went charging in the front door of the house carrying two bags of groceries—so along with my hurry, I could not see over the bags. One of the kids had left the piano bench sitting out well into the room (a little thing left undone), and I went sprawling. I was immobilized for most of a week with an injured knee. Patty brought dinner one night: a gourmet casserole, tossed salad, and a beautifully decorated cake—and to top it all, flowers for the table. Not only did Patty's creativity tell me she cared enough to spend an entire day in the kitchen just for me—her thoughtfulness inspired my lagging appetite and low spirits caused by the pain medication.

At other times the language of little things is spoken best in the practical, without too many frills. (I know this right now because my sister who is living with us temporarily has done all the "crummy" little things for me like cleaning house, doing laundry and so forth, while I'm finishing this book.)

One of my friends told me about the practical of little things. She'd been widowed when her children were toddlers. She was stunned with grief, unable to even notice, let alone do, the ordinary tasks necessary to maintain the house and care for the kids. She received many expressions of concern and sympathy—cards, letters, flowers, contributions to the memorial fund. But when she surfaced from the shock of her husband's death, those were not the things that meant the most to her. Most meaningful was the expression of care by a woman friend who moved in, fed the kids, washed the dishes and did the laundry. So quietly were the practical little things carried out that my friend did not even notice for two days that the helper was there.

Being there is a very important "word" in the language of friendship. By being there, I mean being available for what a friend needs. Availability speaks a special message: I care enough for you that I will do whatever I am able whenever you need me. Saying that might change a friend's life. It changed Joe's.

I met Joe at a conference. He is a genuinely nice person,

and I liked him right away. As the week of the conference progressed, we had quite a few good talks. He told me how much availability had meant to him.

Joe's back went out and he had a lot of pain. As the pain persisted, he began to suffer mentally, too. He couldn't work, and lost confidence in himself.

He went to see his pastor, a well-known and respected teacher of Bible and psychology in the area where Joe lives. It might have been humorous, Joe said, if he hadn't *needed* someone to listen and care. The pastor immediately went into his counseling routine, almost as if he were putting on his white coat. Not asking what Joe wanted or needed, the pastor grabbed a slip of paper and drew a circle, divided into parts of life. He then proceeded to tell Joe which part of life he needed help in and which ones he, the pastor, could help with. He offered to get Joe a part-time job, but his main observation was that when Joe got his spiritual life together, his back and his job would be no problem. All this without listening first to Joe. Joe felt he was getting a "canned" response: Everyone with a spiritual problem got lecture #32, those with marital problems got #34 and so forth. Even worse, the pastor avoided Joe after that visit. Joe's phone calls, which were about unrelated topics and not excessive, certainly—three in two months—were not returned. And when Joe finally walked up to say hello to his pastor one Sunday after worship service, there was obvious embarrassment, followed by obvious relief when Joe didn't ask to talk about his problem.

On the other hand, a friend, a lay Bible teacher, made himself available to Joe. "I'd considered we were friends before that," Joe said. "But that night when I went to him, he proved he meant it. I knew he would do anything he could, and that anything he had was mine.

"My friend was busy," Joe said, "but he found time to be

with me. I saw that he was a true Christian—he showed it in his actions and not just by words."

What Joe's friend actually *did*, was just be there. Joe talked, he listened. He suggested Bible passages Joe might read, and scripture began to come alive and have meaning. While reading Romans 12:1, Joe wondered why God would want a body like his that was so messed up with physical pain. That intrigued him.

Reading scripture like this, together with his friend's availability, influenced Joe to decide to give his life to Christ. The experience changed his life in another way: Joe wants to begin a Christian counseling program in his area. The counselors, he says, will be highly trained, but more important, they will be available to meet each person where his needs are.

Availability, or any of the words in the language of little things, might mean a long-term investment: standing by.

I love reading through the Old Testament stories, because sometimes something just bounces off the page at me. This happened with "standing by" one day when I was reading Ezra.

Ezra 5:2 says that Zerubbabel and Jeshua ". . . arose and began to rebuild the house of God which is in Jerusalem; and with them were the prophets of God, helping them." (RSV)

What kind of help? It seems to me that Zerubbabel and Jeshua were the ones who must have known what they were doing concerning the building process. They were the craftsmen, the guys who could look at the plans and follow them. The prophets were gifted in other ways. Though perhaps they could offer some slight assistance, I'll bet some of them couldn't put one stone on top of another for the actual work of rebuilding. I think those prophets were there with the builders mostly to be supportive. The help they were giving was standing by.

This kind of standing by, being supportive, is a beautiful

part of being friends. When a person is in a crisis or involved
in a situation that takes a period of time to resolve, it's not
enough to offer help and then run off, as if their need were
taken care of. What we do at a time like this might not be so
important as just the fact that we're standing with our friend
while she works on the problem. Sometimes this just means
enjoying having her around when she's suffering, affirming her
and giving encouragement.

This was made personal for me a couple years ago when I
felt really angry with my church because of a misunderstanding concerning some church politics. It was a tough
place to be, because the church community which had meant
so much to me now seemed to be cut off from me, and I felt
like an outsider. I kept getting more and more angry until I
finally just did not attend worship services or anything else for
a long time. When it appeared that no one missed me, I was
really feeling frustrated and unimportant! But there were
some church friends who stood by me during this time—
almost as if they refused to cut me out of their lives or to
allow me to cut them out of mine. They listened to my rant-
ings and ravings, and just encouraged me while I struggled. It
was a beastly struggle, too. I looked into myself, I cried, I
fought, I decided I would forgive, or else! It didn't work. The
healing finally came, not through the intensity of my own
efforts to resolve my problem, but through the standing by of
my few friends. One evening as we stood together in a circle,
I suddenly realized that this little group of friends standing
around me, caring about me and affirming me in spite of my
lashings out against the church—*was* the church. I saw that
my struggle had been against the institution, and not against
the real Body of Christ. This made me free to understand that
*I* was a large part of the problem with the church. I had done
any cutting off that had occurred. The political disagreement
had long since been forgotten by everyone but me. I had let it

affect my relationship to the rest of the Body. With the help of those friends who had stood by me and not let me be cut off entirely, I was able to resolve my anger, forgive and get back into the church.

Probably one of the most important words in the language of little things is "play": having fun with our friends. Yet we find this difficult to do. The old Protestant work ethic has caused us to take life so seriously that we believe we need to be working and producing all the time. And heaven forbid that we even think of enjoying the work or the producing. We tend to look at all of life as something we *have* to do.

At worst, we view play as something that is an escape from reality. It's okay for children, but must be put aside when we grow up. The adult who has fun on his job, or spends time engaging in playful activities, is thought of as a child in adult's clothing. We maintain that play is frivolous, something we don't need, and to have fun, especially too much fun, is being self-indulgent.

At best, we accept play as being a diversion from work. We plan periods of recreation, often using the creation story of the seventh day as a kind of justification. But the recreation is usually some *planned* activity, sometimes only on Sunday, and whether or not it is fun is secondary to the fact that it is structured and metered out as a reward. Another acceptable form of diversion that we sometimes consider play, is relaxation—which, in other words, means sitting, sometimes almost comatose, doing nothing. That's fun?

We've even carried our misconceptions about play into our interpretation of Jesus. We've looked at the serious side of His ministry, and have so thoroughly avoided anything smacking of playfulness that we may read all through the Gospels many times without seeing humor and fun in Jesus. (I know this because I've done that very thing.) But if we look closer, there

are things indicating Jesus did enjoy having fun. For one
thing, He seemed to love parties, and anyone who loves parties
can't be all serious.

Being too serious myself is one of the things that has made
it difficult for *me* to see that Jesus had a sense of humor and
liked fun. Only in the past few years am I discovering that I
do have a sense of humor, buried under all the deadpan expression stuff.

Seeing *Godspell* helped me to see Jesus' playfulness. Author
John-Michael Tebelak portrayed Christ as a clown. Jesus
comes across so affectionate and fun-loving with His friends
that it touched me deeply. I went back to see it twice and
took the kids the second time—I didn't want them to miss seeing a different side to Jesus' personality. *Godspell* gave me
new ideas about play—and changed my conceptions about
what the historical Jesus was like.

Since the historical Jesus is the same Jesus who lives in us,
as the Holy Spirit, it makes a lot of sense to me that we have
not only God's permission, but His encouragement to have fun
together, to take pleasure in being together.

The first requirement, I think, is to change our concept of
the word pleasure. Pleasure has had a rather negative connotation: Pleasure-seekers are those who try to escape or avoid
work. To seek pleasure in that way doesn't work because it's
forced. There's a kind of "you will have fun today or else" attitude that results from spending one's life *trying* to play.
That's boring, maybe even drudgery.

But I think we all need to become pleasure-seekers in another way, by seeking ways to play with our friends. Play
doesn't necessarily mean freedom from work—it may even be
a part of work.

That play doesn't mean freedom from work is evident by
some of the activities considered to be recreational. Many
sports take more energy, more giving out, more work, than

anything else we do. I've learned that by swimming: I have to do seventy-two lengths of the pool for my mile. And swimming is less exhausting than other sports like running. (I love to tell my running friends that swimming is more fun!)

Sailing, too, pointed out to me that pleasure can be found in something that is actually work. From the beach, the sailboats out there in the harbor appear to just skim effortlessly over the water. Sailing with our friends *was* marvelously effortless —I just flaked out and soaked up the sun. But when we joined a sailing club and began sailing ourselves, I discovered that hoisting sails and trimming jibs is a lot of hard work. Plus, it increases everyone's appetite, meaning more food preparation work for me on the days we sail! But that hard work has given our family a lot of pleasure over the past two years.

The ideal, in learning to play, then, is not to seek to avoid work or to play all the time, but to seek pleasure in all that we do.

It's kind of a joke on us that we who are so affluent and have so many *things,* need to learn how to play. But rather than learning something new, learning to play is really just allowing ourselves to let playfulness seep back into our lives. It's a "giving ourselves permission" kind of thing. We all remember *how* to play from childhood. The child we once were still lives within. Some of us have gotten the idea that we need to keep that kid under lock and key, and not let him or her out for fear of looking immature. But play gives that little kid a way of expression and keeps our child from throwing a tantrum when we least expect it. Rediscovering the playfulness in us means heading into life with anticipation and imagination, seeking surprises—like a child. Doing this will make us, as adults, more fun for anybody to be with—and a pleasure to our friends.

Although play, like the other little things, may seem not really necessary, it does add a dimension to friendship. Doing things together that are pleasurable helps us as friends to know each other more completely. And an attitude of playfulness might really brighten a friend's day: It says we care enough for our friend that we *seek* ways to find pleasure being together with him.

One reason an attitude of playfulness is great is because it tends to simplify our complex schedules. Usually, for example, with our couple friends, we make plans way ahead of time to do something. This means telephone calls, checking out everyone's schedule, and rearranging the date at least twice. But recently, our friend Walt just called one Saturday night and said, "Let's go to a movie." Fifteen minutes later, we'd dressed and were on our way. It was a break in a hectic weekend, simple and enjoyable, and it let us know Walt enjoys our company—all because he allowed his playfulness to express itself.

Playing together, for those of us distant from relatives, may be a way to enjoy an adopted extended family. Some of my friends have come up with beautiful ways to encourage the formation of an adopted extended family. The most important ingredient is play. Last year we went on a pumpkin hunt at Halloween: A bunch of families with kids aged two to seventeen, got together, drove to the pumpkin farm, turned the kids loose while adults bought nuts and fruitcake supplies—and then ended the day with a picnic.

But there doesn't have to be a holiday to have fun with friends in the form of an adopted family. Patty and I just made a holiday up this summer—a "Celebrate Summer" beach picnic. Again we got together the gang of families—but this time added some singles and a couple of grandmothers. What fun!

Learning to speak the language of little things—expressing care and concern—is a *big* part of being friends. Carving out time for one another from our frantic schedules is one of the most difficult parts of making and keeping friends. If a friendship depends on quantity of time available, it probably won't happen—there never will be enough time.

Little things give us a way around this problem of time, for in the final analysis, being friends means cherishing not how *much* of a friend's time we have, but instead how that time is spent. Little things—the stuff friendship is built on—add the dimension of quality to all our interactions with friends. The moments we spend together will be precious ones.

# ELEVEN

## Being a Servant:
## Finding the Balance

One of the things most difficult for me to learn while swimming is that I cannot be piggish about breathing. If I take big, gulping breaths of air, I can barely swim one lap. I end up at the end of the pool every few minutes, tired out, panting. And I get out of the pool after my swim, feeling exhausted, rather than refreshed.

If, instead, I breathe in gently and then breathe out what *seems to be more* air than I've taken in, I can swim lap after lap without feeling the least bit tired. And I get out of the pool after my mile feeling revived rather than worn out.

The times when I get piggish about breathing, I've discovered, are when I am somehow afraid that I will not get enough oxygen. I want to get, and then keep all I get. In doing so, I do myself in. Holding in too much air causes my respiratory muscles to tire. And not breathing out enough keeps the waste products of exercise, carbon dioxide and lactic acid inside my body, preventing the oxygen that I do need from getting in and doing its work. My body is all out of whack—unbalanced.

Learning to breathe properly has taken concentration and

training and still, after a year of effort in that direction, requires that I work constantly for balance. And the secret of balance is that it *does* feel as if I'm giving out more than I'm taking in. Other swimmers have told me they experience the same thing.

Thus, while it is actually physiologically impossible to breathe out more than I breathe in—my *perception* of the balanced intake and output is that the giving out seems to require more effort and energy than the breathing in. It seems as if I'm always giving out and seldom taking in.

And that's exactly the way it is in being a servant. To find the proper balance between serving a friend and being served in return, means that it will probably *feel* as if we're giving more than what we're getting. But when the balance is correct, being a servant will be a joy—revive and refresh us rather than wear us down.

Finding the balance in being a servant is much more difficult than finding the breathing balance for swimming. But the reason we fail to serve our friends is the same reason we fail in swimming: We are afraid that we won't have enough for ourselves. We want to get and keep what we get.

With that concentration on self and taking in, we will never be able to serve a friend other than for a brief time or in a surface manner. And this giving just briefly and superficially will wear us out. We'll always be at the end of our "emotional pool," panting for breath.

But there are more serious consequences than emotional exhaustion when we concentrate on taking in rather than giving out: Our ability to make friends and to keep them will be drastically limited. Not being able to serve means that we will find it impossible to fully put into action all the rest of the back-door strategies. A basic underlying attitude of servanthood is absolutely necessary to get inside the back door of a friend's life. And like learning to breathe properly while swimming, it takes training, and effort. I must concentrate on others. That means that my goals are not set on *having* friends, but on *being* one. It means I regard myself as no longer belonging just to me. I belong to my friends.

I must consciously choose servanthood. As I read John 18, where Jesus called His disciples—His friends—servants, and talked about His kingship not being of the world, I got some insight about the difference in serving because one wants to, as opposed to earthly royal kingdoms where there is forced servanthood. Just as wanting to is the key to being a servant of Jesus, we must want to serve our friends. To be a servant is a privilege we can choose, not a have-to that's put upon us.

Consciously choosing might mean taking a look at the things in our lives that keep us from wanting to serve our friends. For me, one of those things is busyness.

Busyness is tricky. Sometimes it looks as if I'm serving others with all my activities and running about. Some of my busyness does serve family and friends. But what looks like service may not be. My busyness often gets carried to extremes. When that happens, it is a form of me-ness that so takes up my time and energy that I am not free to be truly a servant of others.

Another form of me-ness that keeps me from wanting to serve my friends is my introspection. It's a kind of looking at life inside out, seeing all the seams, hems and wrong side of the garment's fabric. This causes me to be more interested in myself and what I am up to than I am in my friends. I've missed out on knowing a number of fascinating people just because of my self-interest. Wanting to serve means that I have to retrain myself to look at the outer view, what my friend needs from me.

Once we've chosen to be a servant and have decided to retrain ourselves to *want* to serve our friends—*how* we do that serving is important. The how is important because there are two ways to serve, and only one has a lasting effect on the friendship.

The first and least effective way to serve is to do so in a reserved manner. This means being afraid to give too much for fear of being worn out. Serving, but still protecting self, as if we might run out of stuff to give. Even though we put forth the effort, the restricted manner in which we give means that our friend will not be very well served.

Real servanthood means not holding back: abandoning self to the friendship with enthusiasm; putting everything I am, unreservedly, into being a friend. One result of not holding back is that it's contagious: Friends catch it from friends.

Something wonderful happens in our friend's life if we are able to abandon self and serve with enthusiasm. It is almost as if we become a catalyst in that person's life, speeding the processes of her growth and helping her to be more fully herself. That, in turn, enables her to go out and serve *her* friends without holding back. Someone else catches the enthusiasm from her, and so it goes, friend after friend, serving one another without reservation.

To serve without reservation doesn't mean without limitations, however. The first limitation concerns our personhood. As Andrew Greeley says, ". . . a doormat cannot be a friend." He goes on to say:

We give ourself to each other in friendship without condition or reservation but, at the same time, we draw a line around ourself which we refuse to let anyone cross, even the friend; one might say, especially the friend. . . . When we impose limitations on our friends we are, in effect, simply making the most important demand that we can make, and that is the demand that the friend respect the integrity of our selfhood. We will gladly yield ourselves to him in complete surrender so long as we yield ourself as human beings, with dignity and integrity; but if he demands that we give up our integrity, our privacy, our freedom, and belong so totally to him that we become not more than human but less than human, we must bluntly refuse.[1]

If a friend is so possessive of us that he makes demands that lessen us as persons, it is not selfish or non-serving to refuse. It is only as we are fully ourselves, whole human beings, that we have the ability to be a servant. So, to refuse to allow a friend to intrude upon our personhood is actually as much for his benefit as it is for our own good. Maybe more.

Another limitation concerns the number of close friends we have. Carving out time to spend with a few special friends increases the potential for depth and endurance of friendship. Jesus did this when He selected the twelve; He ministered to all, but the twelve were special. Just so, we may have many superficial friendships, but limiting the number of special friends is necessary. This does not mean we should cut others out of our life. It simply means we can be more inclusive with a few friends. Rather than lessening our ability to serve, this means that we will be more able to serve *all* people because we have been nourished and filled by a few very special friendships. We will have much to give, even to the most casual of friends.

A third kind of limitation concerns conserving our energies and working for "distance," rather than overextending our physical and spiritual limits. For example, when a swimmer sprints, he uses oxygen faster than his lungs can absorb it. This means that he must borrow oxygen from the blood and muscles and is called "oxygen debt." (I've never been able to swim fast enough to worry about oxygen debts!) An oxygen debt, like all other debts, has to be repaid. The swimmer who overextends his body can do so for only a brief time, and then must stop to rest. While there may be times in serving a friend when we must overextend and borrow energy for a crisis, that energy must always be repaid. We'll have to rest afterward. It is important that we learn to know our limits—and be able to differentiate the distance situation from the crisis— and then *pace* our energies so that we might be able to serve our friend on a continuing basis. Otherwise, we may be out of energy, resting, just when a friend needs us most.

Being a servant means something different to each one of us because we are gifted in different ways. Spiritual gifts may appear to be limitations when we look at them from the wrong side and wish for more than we have.

But seen from the proper viewpoint, gifts are liberating rather than limiting because we do not have to feel responsible to serve *all* the needs of a friend. We can't help everyone in every circumstance. We are able to focus our ministry to our friends and serve out of our own giftedness rather than feeling forced to do everything.

To do this we must know what our gifts are. Don Williams, when teaching a class at our church, said that discovering spiritual gifts requires several steps:

First, study the scripture verses that mention gifts, such as Rom. 12:6–8, I Cor. 12:4–11, and Eph. 4:11. Next, be open to what God gives rather than looking for some specific gift. The third step is to ask a friend who knows us well what he thinks our gift might be. Looking backward at our life as a Christian is helpful because the hindsight might provide clues or reveal something about the nature of our gifts. Finally, Don says, we discover our gifts as we use them to serve others.

To serve others. That's the real reason for spiritual gifts. Eph. 4:12–16, says that gifts are for the equipment of the saints, to build the Body, and to help us grow in Christ. That means to me that we are to search for the gifts that will minister to our friends for that purpose—and, that we needn't look for big and splashy gifts.

Some of the bigger gifts are nice to have, too, and they minister in special ways. But if we look at the circulatory system in the human body, we see a hint of where the real work is done. It's easy to give the credit to the major veins and arteries because they carry the blood to its destination. But when it comes to getting the food and oxygen supply to the individual cells—it's the little, seemingly insignificant, capillaries that do the work. Without capillaries, the veins and arteries are useless, and, without the little, comfortable, everyday kinds of spiritual gifts that minister to individual needs, the big and spectacular ones might just as well not be. The gifts to desire, for friendship, are the ones that enable us best to serve our friends in practical ways.

Jesus served in practical ways. It took me a while to catch the meaning of that, though. I always puzzled over the story of Jesus washing the disciples' feet. The story didn't seem terribly significant to me, and I even wondered why it was included in the Bible. But then one day the meaning became clear.

I saw that my misunderstanding was caused mainly by my focus on modern conveniences. With daily showers, comfortable shoes and easy transportation, feet aren't too much trouble. But, it takes hurting feet to understand just what Jesus did.

When I was taking a class at San Diego State, one day I arrived too late to park in the nearest lot. Even the near lot is quite a walk to class, with steps to climb. But the alternative, the lot where I had to park that day, is so bad that it's called "The Pits." I counted the steps: 201.

I'd worn new shoes—the kind with the toes cut out. By the time I got to class, I had blisters on the top of all ten toes. As soon as class was over, I split for the bookstore and bought Band-Aids. But the blisters were so bad that they kept rubbing even through the Band-Aids. So, I removed the shoes and walked barefoot down the steps and the half-mile to my car. And burned the bottom of my feet on the hot pavement! It was that night, sitting with my feet soaking in warm

water, that the story of Jesus washing the disciples' feet became more than just a symbolic gesture of servanthood to me.
*Now* I could picture the disciples, tired from a long walk.
Their feet hurt, and when feet hurt, the whole body is misera-
ble. When Jesus stooped to wash those feet, it was not just
*symbolic* of being a servant. It was a practical and loving
thing to do, something that really ministered to the needs of
tired men. Understanding this taught me to look for simple
and practical, rather than spectacular, ways to serve my
friends.

Even when simple and practical, being a servant may be
costly. It might mean that at times we need to relinquish our
rights, and as Lewis Smedes says:

Seeking "our own" is built into our system, and for the most part
Christians are card-carrying members of the "self-seekers" club.[2]

To relinquish our rights isn't easy. That's because we are
giving up what we justly deserve—what belongs to us. Our first
reaction is to scream, "Mine, mine!" When serving a friend
means letting go of what is rightfully ours, we might wish that
we hadn't made the choice to be a servant!

It helps to look at Christ: ". . . who, though he was in the
form of God, did not count equality with God a thing to be
grasped, but emptied himself, taking the form of servant,
being born in the likeness of men." (Phil. 2:6–7, RSV.)

Now, *that* is relinquishing rights! If Jesus, who deserved
and had everything, gave up His position with God in order to
serve humanity, perhaps we could give up a right or two now
and then for a friend.

Of course, the preliminary to relinquishing rights means
knowing what rights we have. Defining rights is necessary so
that we don't just unconsciously give in to all the desires of
other people and let them trample us. That is an unhealthy
giving up of rights and leads to resentment. Defining what is

rightfully ours, even if that means taking a course in assertiveness training, is the first step. Then we can consciously step away from our rights, if necessary, for the sake of a friend.

There are times when we may actually *seek* our rights and still serve. Lewis Smedes listed three situations where this is true:

1. When it helps someone else to get his rights.
2. When it is necessary so that I can do the task God has given me.
3. So that I am treated with dignity and respected as God's child and partner.[3]

Each of these situations is consistent with being a servant. The first is quite direct, seeking my rights that my friend might have hers. The third I've already mentioned while discussing limitations.

But what about the second? What difference does doing my task make where *serving* my friend is concerned? Smedes suggests that our tasks were given to us by God not for our good, but for the good of everyone. Therefore it is important for everyone that we do not neglect our stewardship of the job God has assigned.

We need to focus on that job, as Nehemiah did while rebuilding the Jerusalem wall, and shout with him: "I am doing a great work and I cannot come down. Why should the work stop while I leave it and come down to you?" (Neh. 6:3, RSV.)

Nehemiah would not allow distractions to interrupt his work. When our priorities are that straight, and we stand and put God's work first, we won't have to wonder about serving our friend. Being a servant will be part of God's work for us and will fit into the pattern. Seeking our rights for God's task will actually mean seeking our rights to serve a friend.

Being a servant doesn't just cost where rights are concerned. It hits us even deeper, right down to the core of our being.

Serving costs because it means making myself vulnerable to my friend. That means open—susceptible—to being hurt. To serve a friend in a way that ministers to her needs, requires a kind of surrendering of all that I am, trusting her not to "get" me in the process. And because she is human, and I am too, at times I'll feel that she did get me. That hurts. I can only take the risk of making myself vulnerable if I believe there is something beyond myself giving me stability and reliability.

Sailing taught me what it means to have stability and reliability. When I first took sailing lessons, I was terrified every time the boat tilted. I'd seen plenty of small sailboats tip over in the bay, and even though I was sailing a much larger one, I was certain that sooner or later the boat would tip, turn upside down, and dunk me (that's why I learned to swim!). But when I explained my fears to the instructor, he told me how the boat was built. A keel-type sailboat has a built-in reliability. A huge lead keel below the water adds weight and stabilizes the boat. Even if the wind overpowers it temporarily, tilting it sideways, the boat never turns upside down or goes under. As soon as the wind spills from the sails, the boat automatically rights itself. I don't think I want to tilt over far enough to test the boat's reliability—I'll just believe my sailing instructor. But knowing the boat has a built-in reliability is a great comfort to me while sailing.

Knowing that this kind of built-in reliability is available to me in my life is an even greater comfort. Christ, in my life, becomes a stabilizer just like the keel on the boat. With Him, I can take the risk of being vulnerable with my friend. If things get rough, I may tilt a little in the process, but I'll never go under. With Christ as keel, I have a built-in reliability that sets me upright through anything.

But, stability is not the only reason I need Christ in my life if I am to be a servant. On my own, I may make the choice and seek to minister to the needs of my friends. I might make some progress in the right direction, even learn the limitations and how to relinquish my rights. But I will never find the proper balance to the giving out and taking in because my perception is distorted to make it feel as if I'm giving more than I'm getting. Going it alone, I'll always have the intake and the output out of whack—unbalanced. Being a servant will be drudgery.

That unbalance can only be corrected as Christ lives in me and teaches me how to serve. What better teacher could I have, than One who came to serve?

From Christ, I learn the secret of balance in being a servant: With His power lined up beside my desire to serve, I need not be piggish about the intake, and I'll never be at the end of my "emotional pool." I can leave the balance to Him, and take joy from the giving, with no holding back.

Giving, being a servant to our friends, is basic to implementing all the back-door strategies. Only as we have an attitude of serving can we give enough to get inside a friend's life and make a difference because we are there.

And why is giving so important?

Because friendship itself is a gift. Being friends is not just a quickly thought of idea or magical scheme to get us breezily past our loneliness. Friendship is part of God's plan for the empty spots we have inside—the ones He put there Himself when He created us.

When God gave us, through Jesus Christ, the methods of making friends and keeping them, too, He gave us a very precious gift: the gift of each other.

# Notes

## CHAPTER TWO

1) Brenton, Myron, *Friendship* (New York: Stein and Day, 1974), p. 17.

## CHAPTER THREE

1) Jourard, Sidney, *The Transparent Self, Self Disclosure and Well-Being* (Princeton, N.J.: D. Van Nostrand Company, Inc., 1964), pp. 107–8. Italics mine.
2) Greeley, Andrew M., *The Friendship Game* (Garden City: Doubleday & Company, Inc., 1970), p. 156.

## CHAPTER FOUR

1) Womack, Ellie, *The Wall Street Journal*, "PEPPER . . . and Salt," July 19, 1974. Used by permission.
2) Kuglin, John, San Diego *Union*, "Seldom in the Dark," December 9, 1975, AP.

## CHAPTER SIX

1) Hodge, Marshall Bryant, *Your Fear of Love* (Garden City: Dolphin Books, Doubleday & Company, Inc., 1967), p. 139.

## CHAPTER SEVEN

1) Guder, Eileen L., *The Many Faces of Friendship* (Waco, Tx: Word Books, 1969), p. 98.

2) Buechner, Frederick, *Wishful Thinking, A Theological ABC* (New York: Harper & Row, Publishers, 1973), p. 2.
3) Carlisle, Thomas John, *You! Jonah!* (Grand Rapids: William B. Eerdmans Publishing Company, 1968), p. 42. Used by permission.
4) Buechner, Frederick, op. cit., pp. 28–29.
5) Tillich, Paul, *The Eternal Now* (New York: Charles Scribner's Sons, 1963), p. 32.

## CHAPTER EIGHT

1) Tournier, Paul, *The Meaning of Persons* (New York: Harper & Row, Publishers, 1957), p. 161.

## CHAPTER NINE

1) This is discussed in *Theological Dictionary of the Bible,* edited by Gerhard Kittel and Gerhard Friedrich, translated by Geoffrey W. Gromiley, D. Litt, D.D. (Grand Rapids: William B. Eerdmans Publishing Company, 1971), p. 123.

## CHAPTER ELEVEN

1) Greenley, Andrew M., op. cit., pp. 102–3.
2) Smedes, Lewis B., *Love Within Limits* (Grand Rapids: William B. Eerdmans Publishing Company, 1978), p. 38.
3) Ibid., pp. 39–41. (Not direct quotes.)